THE

F!NN!SH

L!NE

MORE F!NNFUN

by

Bernhard H!ll!la

To my parents
Hugo and Hannah Hillila
to whom I owe my love of Finnishness

Acknowledgments

Portions of the material in this book were delivered as lectures during my 1997–98 tenure as "Performer of the Year" for the Finlandia Foundation. Some portions have been previously published in the journal *New World Finn*.

The poems "At the Café Engel," "Grandfather Eino," and "My Grandfather's Watch" were originally published in *New World Finn*; the poems "Sulo" and "On a Roll" were previously published in *Connecting Souls: Finnish Voices in North America*; the poem "Waist" was originally published in *Spirits*.

— Bernhard Hillila

Books by Mail
$14.95 *Finnish Touches: Recipes and Traditions*
$10.95 *Finnish Proverbs* translated by Inkeri Väänänen Jensen
$ 6.95 *Fine Finnish Foods* (This book only $9.95 postpaid;
        small 160 page recipe-card-file size, spiral bound)
$12.95 *Suomi Specialties: Finnish Celebrations* by Sinikka Grönberg Garcia
$12.95 *Words of Wisdom and Magic from the* Kalevala translated by
        Richard Impola
$12.95 *FinnFun* by Bernhard Hillila
$12.95 *THE F!NN!SH L!NE: MORE F!NNFUN* by Bernhard H!ll!la
Complete catalog including all Finnish titles: $2.00

(Shipping: $4.95; for orders over $25.00 add $5.95)
Please send personal check, or for credit card orders call 1-800-728-9998.
Penfield Books, 215 Brown Street, Iowa City, Iowa 52245

ISBN 0-9717025-8-6   LCCN 2002104646
Library of Congress   © 2002 Bernhard Hillila

About the Author

If clothes make the man, Bernhard Hillila has been somewhat of a work in progress! After diapers and school clothes, he has subscribed to different dress codes. He has donned a Lutheran pastor's vestments in bilingual congregations of the Suomi Synod and put on the doctoral hood and other academic regalia of a professor and university administrator at Suomi College (now Finlandia University), Hamma School of Divinity (now Trinity Seminary), California Lutheran University, and Valparaiso University; he has worn the proper suit and tie of Finlandia Foundation's "Performer of the Year," the casual attire of a poet and stand-up comedian, and the elk-soled pigskin shoes of an accomplished wire walker. Since he's so very Finnish, there must have been many times when he went to a sauna and didn't wear any of those outfits!

Currently professor emeritus of education at Valparaiso University, Hillila still is somewhat of a cross-dresser—preaching sermons, giving lectures, performing comedy skits, and conducting poetry workshops. He is listed in *Who's Who in America* not for his sartorial elegance but for his other accomplishments. While writing this, his ninth book, Bernie may have worn a clown suit or a court jester's garb!

David Fitzsimmons, editorial cartoonist with the *Arizona Daily Star* in Tucson since 1985, was a finalist in the 1988 Pulitzer awards. He is a celebrated speaker, commentator, respected standup comedian, and community and professional leader in the Tucson area. David and lovely Finnish wife Anne Halttunen, niece of author Bernhard Hillila, are the parents of daughter Sarah, son David Alexander Armas, and son Matthew Madison Fitzsimmons, a new arrival in 2002.

Table of Contents

Introduction

I'm no scientific authority on Finnishness. Those wishing a scholarly discussion of matters Finnish should subscribe to the *Journal of Finnish Studies* or take a course in Fennistics, the study of the Finnish language.

My approach is somewhat like Russell Snyder's in his book, *The Lighter Side of Finland*, a "survival guide" published in 1996. He had lived in Finland for fifteen years and reported that "There is more than enough here to keep me captivated, delighted, charmed and sometimes puzzled. It has been said that Finns lack a sense of humor, but I know that Finns love to laugh and are quite happy to joke about themselves."

I'm just an observer. But I *am* a Finn—that helps! I'm Finnish on my parents' side—made in the U.S. with Finnish parts. On one of my visits to Dr. Chiu, our family doctor, I told him that I was Finnish. He said, "I can't give you anything for that!" My grandparents were boat people. And they had bigger boats than the *Mayflower!* Of course, I did go to a "Finnishing" school— Suomi College (now Finlandia University).

Take what you read here with a grain of salt. In my book *FinnFun*, I kidded that Rodney Dangerfield was originally Rauno Vaarapelto (*vaara* = "danger" and *pelto* = "field"). One conscientious reader displayed unfoolable Finnish logic, sending my publisher an article documenting that "Dangerfield" was born Jacob Cohen. Well, if the guy himself doesn't want to use his right name, why should I? The truth of the matter is that his father had originally changed his Finnish name, Jaakko Korhonen, to Jacob Cohen when he came to the U.S.! Now, don't bother doing research on that—I don't want to be confronted with facts when I'm having fun!

— Bernhard Hillila

Inventory of the
Finnish Personality

What are Finns like? First of all, all Finns are blond, blue-eyed, and with small noses. If you doubt that, look at my picture!

No racial or ethnic strain is pure, of course. The Finnish genes have had input from a number of sources. One of the most intriguing illustrations of how a gene pool receives waters from diverse streams is the information that some members of the Finnish Westerinen family of Staten Island, New York, trace their lineage to the youngest son of Black slave Sally Hemmings. Recent high-tech paternity testing has established that Thomas Jefferson fathered at least one child by Hemmings. Dorothy Westerinen is quoted in *Time* (May 24, 1999) as saying, "I'm very proud to share a Black lineage."

Jackie Mason, the Jewish comic, regales audiences with stereotypes of Jewish behavior. Finnish personality stereotypes are less well-known, but let us look at some of them. Although stereotypes are often faulted, they contain a measure of truth. Even in lands far from Finland, Finnish immigrants and their descendants tend to show certain personality traits.

Considering those personality traits, we must remember that there are various combinations of characteristics, and some Finns we know prove that there are exceptions. Even some of the traits are conflicting—for example, we say Finns are extremists, but we also claim Finns have a lot of common sense. You figure it out!

We should also note that not all ethnic crediting is complimentary, as we know from Dutch treating, Scotch spending, Indian giving, Welshing on debts, and so on. Finns, like all humans, are complex packages of good and bad qualities. If all of humanity were Finnish, the world might be cleaner and more poetic, but it could also see more quirky creativity and the bogging down of communication. Thus, the following Finnish traits have both positive and negative aspects.

Shyness

Finns are less outgoing than members of some other nationalities. Just as the Japanese hug less than Americans, so Finns hug less than the Spanish. Being extremely literate, Finns ought to be able to communicate well. In all honesty, however, they tend to be shy and slow to relate to others. There is hesitance to speak, and body language, too, is limited. It's as though some kind of centrifugal force were operating. In a restaurant they go to the tables at the edges or into booths. In a conversation, they drift to the sides, feeling uncomfortable as centers of attraction. Perhaps Finns are "nearing" impaired!

Our son Marty, who is into long-distance running, reports that in Finland, oncoming runners he met almost never made eye contact, whereas in the United States, runners usually acknowledge another runner with a look, a hand-wave, or a "Hi!"

Modest Finns don't take to marketing as easily as some other nationalities. For example, when my subscription to *Newsweek* is scheduled to expire in December, I begin getting renewal notices in June. However, when my subscription to a Finnish publication expires September 17, I get a letter in November informing me that the subscription expired two months earlier. An apology is included, in case I've sent in my subscription since the bill had been sent.

Finns are prone to belittle themselves. Ask a Finn, "Did you sleep well?" and he'll say, "Well, I probably made a couple of mistakes, but I guess I did fairly well!"

Finns in Seattle, Washington, openly recognize this tendency to shyness and chuckle about it. They have a "Finnish Modesty Contest" at the Finn Hall. In the game, contestants are praised for accomplishments. The participants then respond and are judged by the modesty with which they speak. Prizes are given to the winners, who are expected to return them as not being deserved! Thanking for the praise means immediate disqualification. (Hey, I'm so Americanized, praising won't bother me!)

Some Finns work hard to compensate for their shyness. Olavi found it hard to meet people or to start talking to them after he met them. So he'd drive around town until he found a great parking space, then park in it and roll down the window. Soon some lady who hadn't been able to find a space would ask him, "Are you leaving?" And he would say, "Why, yes! Do you want to come with me?"

Koskinen, a shy Finn fellow with romantic intentions, wondered how to approach his cute neighbor. Finally, he asked: "Would you eventually like to be buried in the well-kept Koskinen family plot?"

I know a person who mentioned she had a grandson, a freshman at Whitman College. Her friend asked, "What's he going to be—a pastor, doctor, lawyer?" "Well, I hope he will be a sophomore!"

I had assumed that no self-effacing Finn would apply to appear on the television program "Who Wants to Be a Millionaire," but I noticed a "Kivi" on one of the segments. That name—which means "rock"—is surely Finnish. And more recently, "Mantyla"! Oh, well, it may be that paternal grandfathers were Finnish and the shyness gene had been overwhelmed by other nationalities in the family trees!

Farid Ikene, an exchange student at the University of Tampere, wrote in *The Finnish American Reporter* about his experiences in Finland. He referred to the silence of Finns: "Alfredo, an Italian, mentioned that in the bus people do not say a single word. He said even their babies do not cry in the bus. Valerie, from France, said that people in elevators look in different directions in order to avoid others' eyes." He noted that gestures have a different meaning in Finland than in some other countries: Elizabeth from Spain smiled at her neighbor, who closed her door, afraid that Elizabeth was a lesbian!

Finns are laconic, people of few words. I like Pastor Rudy Seppala's story about Toivo's death. Toivo had never been a good provider, and the arrangements for his burial had to be kept simple. His wife went to the newspaper office and said, "I want you to put a notice in your paper that Toivo has died." She was given a sheet to fill out with wording for the ad, but she protested, "Just put in two words: 'Toivo died.' He was sick a long time, and his friends will get the message." The clerk tried to be helpful, "But you can have five words for the same cost." "Alright then. Put it this way: 'Toivo died—pick-up for sale.'"

During our travels in Finland, we have found even some signs to be timid. At a restricted parking area, instead of being informed that violators will be towed, we read a sign *Pyydämme muuttamaan asianomaiselle pysäköinti paikalle.* (We request you to move to a proper parking space.) Among the signs in tourist hotels were the following: *Eihän täällä tupakoida!* (Surely one wouldn't smoke here!) *Muistithan avaimen?* (You remembered your key, of course!) *Sammutathan valot. Kiitos!* (You'll turn out the light won't you? Thank you!)

Although shy, Finns like to be held in esteem—modest esteem. An elderly, shy parishioner was pleased when a new senior pastor *(rovasti)* named Holopainen was installed at her church. She gathered all her courage and sought him out after the first service: "My name is Holopainen, too—Alma. I wonder if we could be related." The pastor looked at her condescendingly and said, "Oh, well, perhaps through Adam." She responded enthusiastically, "Oh, was his name Holopainen too?"

Shyness can, of course, deteriorate to patterns of unsociability. Solitude can lead to becoming morose. Garrison Keillor, after listening to some Finnish music on his program, concluded, "I don't have that capacity for gloom."

I believe that Finns are becoming more self-confident as they are better known internationally. They are communicating more clearly that Finns may be silent, restrained, modest, but don't intend to be unsocial, withdrawn, impolite.

Sisu

Finns are noted for that unique combination of determination, courage, and stamina called *sisu*. It is intestinal fortitude—guts.

Juniper berries are used to flavor gin. Is that why Finns are called "juniper people" (*katajainen kansa*)? No, it's because junipers are tough, resilient survivors, not easily trimmed to cubes or balls like some plantings. Folks more likely expect Finns on the TV program "Survivor" than on "Who Wants to be a Millionaire."

How many Finns does it take to change a light bulb? None. Finns aren't afraid of the dark! In Finland, they have it all day long in the winter.

Finns aren't afraid of pain either—for aspirin distributed in Michigan's Upper Peninsula, a line has been added to the instructions: "Adults, take two tablets, but Finns, who are suspicious of life when it's too pain-free, take just one."

Hypochondria is the persistent, neurotic conviction that one is ill, or likely to be ill. Finns suffer instead from the opposite of hypochondria: chondrohypia, which is the assumption that one is well even when suffering illness. "Finnish hypochondriac" would be an oxymoron!

After experiencing a sauna, a non-Finn was perplexed: "If this is your fun, what kind of punishments do you have?"

A good example of Finnish *sisu* is Elias Lönnrot, a medical doctor and compiler of the Finnish national epic *Kalevala*, who logged 12,500 miles (halfway around the globe!), mostly on foot, during the period 1828–45.

Even when work is tiring and painful, Finns tend to remain hard-working, punctual, sturdy employees. They are often workaholics. Even in retirement, it's hard for a Finn to be a leisureholic.

Stoicism

Finns come from a country where they're between a rock and the hard ice. When they draw the line, it's not in the sand—it's in granite! It's no surprise that they are known to be quite unflappable. You may hear one say, "So you think life is hard? Cheer up, it's not permanent!"

There's no Finnish equivalent for "Have a nice day!" In fact, I used that English phrase on an old Finn friend of mine, and he answered, "Sorry, I have other plans!"

Wondering whether he was an optimist or a pessimist, I once asked Kalle whether he would say a glass is half full or half empty. "Vell, if it's medicine, it's still half full; if it's vodka, it's already half empty!" Finns aren't optimists, of course, but they really aren't pessimists either—they are realists. The optimist says the glass is half full; the pessimist says it's half empty; the realist Finn says the glass is twice as big as you need!

Innate toughness engenders a simple acceptance of life's harder experiences. As a youngster, granddaughter Maija went to the doctor to get a series of shots prior to leaving with her family on a round-the-world trip. The doctor cautioned her, "You probably should look away from your shoulder." She countered, "But how would I see what you're doing?"

Consider the case of Jorma, who was visiting relatives in the United States. He was obviously in great pain one morning, unable to keep from grimacing and shedding tears profusely. He didn't want to complain, but after much prodding admitted that he had brushed his teeth with what he thought was toothpaste but must have been something else. It was capsaicin, a peppery arthritis salve!

My wife, Esther, was speaking to Mrs. Springsteen on the telephone: "Sure, I think we can come to a patio supper Saturday." I got her attention, pointing at our schedule book, so she continued: "Oh, no, Bernie reminds me I have an abdominal operation on Thursday."

One Finn who lost a foot to a land mine in the Winter War said philosophically, "Well, stepping on one was better than sitting on one!"

Do you realize that all your parts have a lifetime guarantee? The catch, of course, is that the lifetime may be disappointingly short. My brother-in-law Paul Hartman was a good example. Dying of a brain tumor at the age of forty-nine, he was making one of his frequent visits to the doctor's office; when the doctor asked how things were going, Paul smiled and said, "All I need is a new head!" As he staggered, he added, "And I should probably get more exercise!"

Some years ago, while I was awaiting an operation, my pastor called on me in the hospital. As he left, I said, "I'll be seeing you in church or, if not there, in the hereafter." He was clearly troubled and returned to the bedside to encourage me: "Don't give up!" What was simple Finnish acceptance of options sounded to him like depression and loss of will. He would have been surprised to learn that Finns go to cemeteries at Christmas and that the hymn used so often at funerals, *"Sun haltuus rakas Isäni"* ("Into your care, dear Father"), is a stewardship hymn.

Finns accept the fact that a lifetime may be rather short. Finnish ceramist Karin Widnäs has spoken of a paper urn for burying cremains—human ashes. I resonate to that: the frailty of the urn reminds of the frailty of a human being.

Sense of Humor

In spite of their stoicism, Finns do have a lively sense of humor. Just because they don't smile a lot doesn't mean they're not funny!

At a Finlandia Foundation outing, Shark Finn soup was served, which prompted someone to ask, "Are we going Chinese?" The answer was, "No, it's potato soup, but we call it 'Shark Finn' soup, because the Finnish attorney made it!" By the way, do you know how Finnish lawyers are different? They still charge unconscionable fees, but they feel guilty.

Bystanders once thought they heard a reference to a sea creature: "bottle-nosed dolphin," but it turns out someone was talking about "the bottle-tipping dull Finn."

Jussi and Laila's marriage fell apart, and they settled on a divorce. A year or so later, however, they realized that they really were meant for each other, and that Jussi could give up his drinking, and Laila would no longer nag. They were duly remarried, and at the reception party, surrounded by Finnish friends, self-deprecating Jussi explained things clearly: "I know what you're all thinking—that Jussi couldn't even make his divorce work!"

Perhaps because of their stoic nature, Finns express quite a bit of gallows humor. For example, Pastor Wayne Niemi tells the following story from a few decades back: One day, just about in time for morning coffee, Leander Palkki stopped by to visit two bachelor Finns who lived in the boonies. He saw Eino sitting meditatively at the kitchen table: "How are you, Eino?" Eino replied, "It's not been a good day. The first thing, I went to the well to get water for coffee. I guess my brother Mikko had had a bit too much to drink last night, because I found he'd fallen into the well and drowned. I pulled him out, but he was dead, so I carried him to the shed. Now I have to go to town to see the pastor and the funeral director." Leander looked sympathetic and said, "Well, I suppose you never did get that coffee made?"

Honesty

When Finland paid its war debts promptly and fully, the world noted that procedure as rather unique. Finns still value honesty. On our most recent visit to Finland, we found to our amazement that many bikes were left unlocked in public places, as at the train station in Turku!

Have you ever heard of any Finnish entrepreneurs giving illegal campaign contributions to a political party in order to promote saunas and *silakkas* (Baltic herring)?

The day before our family was to return home from a Finland trip, we turned in the car at AVIS in Helsinki, showing the office manager a small scratch we had gotten on the side of the vehicle. Instead of blaming us for the minor damage, he apologized that we had to be standing outside in the gentle rain—just about the only rain we saw in Finland during that trip!

That story doesn't end there. At about 6:00 a.m. when we left the car at the airport lot and had dropped the keys in the slot at the office, we realized we had inadvertently left a poster in the car. Esther wrote a note explaining what had happened and giving our address in the U.S. About a week after we got home, the poster arrived in its mailing tube with about $10 worth of postage paid!

In any nationality, there are exceptions; regarding honesty, we have to take a look at Kankkunen, who was hired by Garden Suppliers. On his first day with the firm, Conk was checked by security guards because he was seen leaving work with a large box in his wheelbarrow. The box proved to be an empty one, perfectly permissible to take, so he was waved on.

Since Conk kept on wheelbarrowing a box out to the parking lot almost every day, the security guys figured, "He's setting us up for a time when he's going to wheel out a box full of expensive Dutch tulip bulbs."

They told the manager they'd continue to check, and they did about every other day, but Conk never had anything illegal.

Kankkunen quit after about a month. Later, in doing inventory, the boss found the employee had stolen over twenty wheelbarrows! The boss just said, "Well, his mother wasn't Finnish!"

Directness

Finns are noted for their directness. It's a Finn thing—just as Finns don't sip liquor, they don't mince words! For example, instead of choosing sauces with fancy French names, Finns gravitate to fried pork gravy (the "biscuits and gravy" kind of gravy), but they're honest about it, calling it *läskisoosi* ("fat sauce")!

Mikko could not tell his telephone answering machine: "I'm not here now." So he was honest and direct in the message he left: "Obviously I am here now, but when you call, I may be gone. If you are a telemarketer, leave your home number where you can be reached at dinner time."

The way the Finns stood up to the giant Soviet Union has made some of them a bit reckless, I'm afraid. Take Ensti, for example, who figured it was about time to take care of that bully Saddam Hussein. He called Saddam: "Hei, hei, Mr. Hussein, this is Ensti in Härmä, Finland. We're declaring war on you!"

"Well, Einstein, how big is your army?"

"Oh, there's me, my brother Eero, my cousin Ville, and the bunch from the ski club."

"Well, Einstein, you should know that I have a million men in my army, ready to fight."

"I'll call you back." The next day he does call: "This is Ensti. The war is still on. The hockey team has joined us, and we've gotten some mechanized equipment for our forces—two combines, a bulldozer, and Mattila's tractor."

"Well, Einstein, you should know that I have 16,000 tanks, 14,000 armored personnel carriers, lots of nerve gas, and my army has increased to one-and-a-half million since we last spoke."

"I'll call you back." He does the next day: "This is Ensti. The war is still on. The guys from the neighborhood talked it over in the sauna, and they've all joined us. And we've gotten airborne— we modified my neighbor Janne's ultralight plane, added a couple of rifles!"

"Well, Einstein, you need to know that I have 10,000 bombers, 20,000 MIG-19 attack planes, laser-guided surface-to-missile sites, and my army has increased to two million."

"Perkele! I'll call you back!" And he does the next day: "Saddama, we're calling off the war."

"Well, Einstein, why are you chickening out?"

"We talked it over here, and there's no way we can feed two million prisoners!"

Creativity

According to George Bernard Shaw, "All progress depends on the unreasonable man." Nut cases in folklore have solved problems in strange ways. Original thinkers today may differ in clothing, habits, and values, express off-the-wall opinions, and generally swim upstream. The innovators and inventors in today's society are persons with creative logic. Thus, creativity underlies the Finnish achievements in both technological inventions and artistic production.

In today's Finland, the original thinker, even the "village idiot" or "nut case" who tangos to a different drummer, is encouraged. The first *Kylähullukonttori* (Nut Case Office) was established in Kemi, Finland, in 1994. This is no laughing matter—the Department of Labor and the City of Kemi back the venture. The annual International Nut Case Festival in Kemi includes all kinds of weird, creative happenings.

For example, what could snowbound Kemi, a town of 25,000 (about the size of Valparaiso, Indiana, but on the northern tip of the Gulf of Bothnia rather than adjoining Chicago on balmy Lake Michigan) do to attract world attention? Well, the most abundant natural resources are snow and ice, so the residents have built a Snow Castle annually since 1996, when the *Guinness Book of Records* listed it as the largest snow castle in the world. Entering the castle through an art gallery featuring Finnish glass art, visitors also view ice sculptures.

In the winter of 1999–2000, the fifth annual castle was built as The Millennium Castle. Constructed over two months as a medieval-style castle with drawbridge, chapel, and snow hotel with restaurant, it required 20,000 cubic meters of tap water.

As a winter visitor to Finland, you'd like an icebreaker? Take the *Sampo*, one of the finest icebreakers in the Gulf!

Once, at the summer hotel Domus in Tampere, we rode an elevator which had a mirror for a ceiling. Since the hotel was a university dormitory during the academic year, the mirror seemed to be designed so that one could look up to the ceiling meditatively and see down the blouses of coeds!

Bonk Business, Inc. was founded by Pär Bonk, who decided he should make machines to make folks happy—not necessarily of any use, but agents of happiness. The Bonk Centre in Uusikaupunki displays hundreds of hilarious machines, products, and articles.

In the United States, kickbikes are becoming more and more popular, along with scooters. But did you know that the kickbike has Finnish roots? In the wintertime—a long period in Finland—Finns used the *potkukelkka* (kicksled) to get around. The sled had a high-backed seat on two wooden runners, which protruded from the rear. A kicksledder could stand with one foot on one of the runners, use the other foot scooter-wise for progress, guide the sled with his hands, and give a ride to a person, groceries, or other carry-ons. Hannu Vierikko, a physiologist, developed the kickbike for similar use. One of the benefits is the use of both legs alternately. In addition to the aerobic workout, kickbiking provides great low-impact exercise for triceps, biceps, forearms, buttocks, quadriceps, and calf muscles.

Cleanliness

Some folks have difficulty with Bible passages that deal with miracles. Finnish mothers have more difficulty accepting passages that do not show a Finnish type of cleanliness, as for example, Mary drying Jesus' feet with her hair or "a praise of oil flowing down from the scalp to the beard!"

Esko said to his new neighbors, "Come over for a bath." That's the way those Finns are. For anyone else, it would be insulting to ask someone to take a bath; but with them, it's a ritual, an extension of hospitality, a way of saying: "We have a sauna and you're welcome!"

Mrs. Luoma had told Eino not to get his new shoes dirty when he went out. He saw the large dog droppings in the yard, picked the mess up in his hands, and ran back into the house: "Ma, look what I almost stepped into!"

Esther got a can of bathroom deodorizer spray with a blueberry scent. It leaves the bathroom quite pleasant, but I don't enjoy biting into her blueberry cobbler as much!

In the spirit of thorough housecleaning, Aino buried her vacuum and her Mixmaster when they died.

Let's consider the ultimate cleansing. Years ago, the late Pastor David Hartman (Halttunen) and I conducted a service, which included a baptism, in Mansfield, Ohio. As the service was about to start, Dave checked the baptismal font and motioned to an usher: "Put some water into the font." The usher looked into the font and answered, "There is some water in there. You don't need very much, do you? Pastor Jones just dipped his finger into the water and made a sign of the cross on the baby's forehead." Dave would have none of that: "I agree we don't need a pool to immerse people in, but we *are* going to baptize them, not dry-clean them! Put in enough water so that it's clear that God washes away our sins."

Logicality

Let me give a few examples from our own family of how Finnish genes can force logic generation after generation.

Esther and I have been married for fifty-seven years. (She must have been a child bride, right?) You probably assume the marriage has lasted because I'm so easy to get along with. No, it has been because of the sheer logic I presented. When we got married, I told her, "If you ever leave me, I'll go with you!"

When sister-in-law Sylvia Soderstrom was organist at Gloria Dei Lutheran Church in Brooklyn, New York, some listener was evidently impressed by her playing: *"Kuinka voisin taata, että soittaisitte minun hautajaisissani?"* ("How could I make sure that you will play at my funeral?") Sylvia's answer was logical: *"No menkää ensin kotiin ja kuolkaa!"* ("Well, go home first and die!")

When our daughter Esther was a little girl, my father, Hugo, tapped her on the head and mused, *"Mitähän tästäkin lapsesta kasvaa?"* She answered, *"Hiuksia!"* ("I wonder what will grow from this little child?" "Hair!")

When I once explained to our daughter Chris that I had to clean my plate so that the food wouldn't go to waste, she asked: "Dad, what makes you think it doesn't go to waste if you eat it?" There's truth as well as a pun in that rejoinder!

The year our grandson Nate started school, our son Marty went to work before Nate left for school. Marty was to call Nate at home at 8:30 a.m. to remind him to get outside to catch the 8:40 school bus. One day at 8:32, Nate called his dad at the office and said, "You're supposed to call me now!"

Finns' logicality means that they generally are not intimidated by nonsense. Olga went to her doctor and came back disgusted: "That doctor doesn't think well. He said the only problem with my right leg is old age. Well, my left leg is just as old, and there's nothing wrong with it!"

When little Antti was asked, "Where did you get those blue eyes?" he answered, "They came with my head!"

Attempting to show how we should not worry about tomorrow but trust in God's care, a pastor asked his confirmation class, "Why do we ask for 'daily bread' instead of 'bread' for several days?" A Finn kid answered, "So it will be fresh!"

Asked to show their visas, a Finnish family pointed to Antti, the wisest (most *viisas)* of the family!

One late-fall night, Oskari was returning home from a tavern and took his usual shortcut through the town cemetery. He didn't know that a grave had been dug that day, right where he used to cut across. He didn't see all that clearly anyway, so he fell into the grave, tried to climb out, but couldn't. He naturally started to call for help. Soon another tipsy guy, Erkki, came along, heard Oskari yelling, looked into the grave, and asked, "What's the matter?" "I want to get out of here!" "Why?" "It's cold." "Well, no wonder—you don't have any dirt on you!"

Have you ever thought how different the Christmas story might have sounded if the gifts to the Child had been brought by three wise women from Finland instead of three wise men from the East?
- They would have asked directions and arrived earlier;
- they would have helped deliver the baby;
- they would have cleaned the stable;
- they would have provided handmade swaddling cloths;

- they would have brought along a rutabaga casserole and rice pudding;
- and they would have brought practical gifts like a mop, a broom, and some deodorizer.

Logic with a Vengeance

When Olli went to Canada, they asked him at the border, "Do you have any firearms?" He answered, "Well, what do you need?"

The party host offered Eero a drink. "I'll have a vodka." "With some tonic water, orange?" "I'll have just a vodka." "Nothing else?" "Well, you can give a glass with it!"

Pastor Wilbert Tormala was once trying to convince an elderly, destitute parishioner to go to the county home, where she would have much better conditions and excellent care. *"No, jos se on niin hyvä, mene itte!"* ("Well, if it's so great, go there yourself!")

Mrs. Pietila was told that a Hoover vacuum cleaner would cut her work in half, so she bought two of them!

Another Finnish lady reprimanded her husband: "How do you expect other people to come to your funeral if you don't go to theirs?"

A fellow named Malmivaara, who had an outstanding father and a son of great promise, ranted drunkenly to his father: "You aren't much of a father. Look at my outstanding son, and look at how rotten your son turned out!"

Consider Esa, who was going about 70 down a state highway when a cop pulled him over and said, "The speed limit here is 55 miles per hour." Esa said, "I know, but I was going to go only half an hour, and it wouldn't be anywhere near that far."

Three Finns were comparing their status. The first said, "I've got a '95 Nissan Maxima." The second said, "I've got a '96 Ford Taurus." As eyes locked expectantly on the third guy, he said, "I guess I've got high blood pressure. I read that every third Finn has high blood pressure!"

When Granddaughter Maija Nelson was about to become a seven-year-old, the family was leaving on a round-the-world trip. Her grandma said, "You'll be celebrating your birthday before you leave, won't you?"

"No, I'll have my birthday in Spain."

"No, I think you'll have it before you leave."

"Grandma, my mother said I'll have my birthday in Spain, and my mother is a Christian woman, so I believe her!"

I don't know what kind of woman she thought her grandma was!

Finns are great on the logic of recycling—archival paper for *ryijy* rugs, old clothes for book covers, telephone directory paper for jewelry. Neighbor kids thought Makela was a recycling nut, so when they t.p.'d his tree, it was with previously used toilet paper!

Of course, even Finns aren't consistently logical—they're human, after all. Otherwise, why would they put the Table of Contents *(Sisällys)* at the end of a book? So the reader can see what was in the volume *after* he's read it?

Quirkiness

When Tauno heard that a thermos can keep hot things hot and cold things cold, he put two cups of coffee and a popsicle in his.

You may have heard the touching comment "I was sad because I had no shoes until I met a man who had no feet." A Finn took the logical next step: "I was sad because I had no shoes until I met a man who had no feet, so I asked him, 'Have you got any shoes you won't be using?'"

Nevala and his wife hadn't been on speaking terms for a couple of days. They communicated by a few notes, like: "The garbage has to go out." Or: "We're out of beer. Get some when you're at the store." One evening Mikko put a note on his wife's pillow: "Wake me at 7:00 in the morning—I have an important meeting." He woke up, noticed it was already 9:00 a.m., but there was a note on his pillow: "Wake up—it's 7 o'clock."

Consider the Finnish curmudgeon Koskenniemi, who filed his income tax in Roman numerals!

Knowing he was on his deathbed, Ahonen whispered to his wife: "Promise me that when I'm gone, you won't remain a lonely widow, but you'll marry Vehanen." "Vehanen? I thought you hated him with a passion." "Exactly!"

Did you hear about Mikkola who, when signing the "Book of Remembrance" for his deceased friend Otto, added his phone number for the widow?

Eero was awakened by the phone one night at 3:00 a.m. His next-door neighbor yelled at him: "Your dog is barking and keeping us awake all night. You better shut him up!" Listening patiently, Eero didn't argue, but at 3:00 a.m. the next night, he called his neighbor and said, "That wasn't our dog!"

Mr. Maki, a public school teacher of Finnish background, was bothered a bit because a girl in his biology class kept dropping things off her desk. The class was studying hormones, and perhaps the girl was just illustrating the topic. A handsome boy on her right picked up a book she had dropped and set it on her desk. She dropped a pencil, which the boy retrieved and gave back to her. Finally, Mr. Maki said logically, "Dave, set all of her stuff on the floor, and hand down anything that falls up!"

Juho was speeding down the highway when he got pulled over by a cop. "Do you know there's a fine for speeding?" "Oh, how much?" "Twenty-five dollars per offense." "OK, give me $100 worth."

No matter how he tried, Aku couldn't make a profit farming in Upper Michigan, so he worked out a deal to work the farm with his brother Saku, who was out of work. "You can work for me for two years, and I'll give you the farm; then I'll work for you for two years, and you can give the farm back to me!"

Eero could be quite gallant. Once the bus was so crowded that his younger teen-age brother had to sit on his lap. At the next stop, a cute gal got on, so Eero said, "Ari, be polite and give the lady your seat!"

Simo ate cheese with prunes to keep his bowel confused, giving it a hard time—or a soft one!

Osmo applied for a job as a writer at the local newspaper. The publisher had been flooded with applications, but he gave the form to Osmo, remarking: "I don't want a lot of pages. I'll take whatever you can put on this one page." Osmo stood on the sheet of paper!

Arvo and Hannu loved their wives, but each one also thought his brother's wife was great. Being religious and morally straight, they never did any wife-swapping, but they once did agree that, if they should die before their wives, they would most likely marry the other one's widow! (Think of the logic of that statement!) They both did pass away before the wives, and the widows never remarried!

There can be a needle in a Finn's comment, as when Tarmo's widow said charitably, "He wasn't always as mean as sometimes!" *("Hän ei ollut aina niin ilkeä kuin joskus!")*

Lots of folks regret that they can't sleep if they drink coffee. Most Finns are sorry they can't drink coffee when they sleep!

I kidded Jaakko about his being a vegetarian, saying that it's not really in the Finnish tradition of *poronpaisti* (baked venison) and *läskisoosi* (drippings gravy). He countered: "You criticize me for being a vegetarian, and I've heard you're a humanitarian!"

At the McKinnon, Georgia, Finnish settlement, the Finnish Hall was registered as a church building to avoid property taxes. Dances, plays, and programs of various kinds were held there, but never a church service!

How do you feel about telemarketers? I don't care if someone has a *doctorate* in telemarketing—I don't want him making house calls. I don't mind being a bit nasty to telemarketers, and my Finnish name makes it easier for me to foil them. For example, the phone rings in the middle of dinner, and I answer.

A sweet voice says, "This is Susie. Are you Mr. Halleluya?"

"No."

"Did I pronounce your name right?"

"No."

"How do you pronounce it?"

"Hill´i-la!"

"Oh, Mr. Hilee´yah, I'm Susie calling from See-Through Window Company."

I say, "Just a moment, Susie. I'll connect you to the department that does windows." Then I put a Sibelius CD on in the background, and Esther and I go on with dinner, once in a while stopping to say, "Please stay on the line. Your call is important to us," or to let Esther say, "Bernie has just had a new book,

FinnFun, published at $12.95, and I'll be happy to take your telephone order now if you have your credit card handy."

Finally, before dessert, Esther gets on the line and says, "Susie See-Through, if you're interested in southern exposure windows, press 1, if it's bay windows like Bernie has, press 2. . . . Oh, shucks, she hung up!"

I personally don't intend to be difficult—it's just my nature. I'm sure I've been difficult for both God and for Esther to live with, although God hasn't mentioned it quite as often!

Frugality

Finns don't like to waste food or leave anything unread in the newspaper. In fact, Finns are so concerned about wasting things that one of them started a museum for the heads and arms from the statues that are in all the other museums.

Real Finns don't throw away perfectly good rags. Nor do they discard the seeds from their tomatoes, no matter what the recipe says.

Finns from Laihia are known as Scotch Finns. Consider Esa, who was informed that the airphone on his plane cost $2.50 for the first minute, $2 for the others. He said he'd take a couple of the "others."

The story is told of a *Laihialainen* who was walking down the sidewalk and spied a penny. A Scot coming from the opposite direction saw it at the same time. That's how copper wire was invented!

You have probably heard that after a wedding in Laihia, only one of the couple goes on the honeymoon.

A couple from Laihia went to eat at a fancy restaurant in Vaasa. They ordered their meals, and the man began to eat. The waiter solicitously whispered to the woman: "Why aren't you eating?" She answered apologetically, "Well, we have only this one pair of false teeth, and I let him eat first!"

A birthday card in Laihia reads, "This card cost less than $1, but you're worth it!"

A Laihia guy considered buying a lounging chair and discovered the chair had a lifetime warranty—so he bought it in his grandson's name.

Finally, Eero from Laihia decided he would end it all, so after he saw the neighbors leave their house, he went over there and turned on their gas, so he wouldn't have to pay for it!

Extremism

We've looked at extreme logicality and extreme frugality. But whatever it is that Finns are, they are extremely that. Perhaps it is natural that Finland, in the extreme north of the world, has a nation of extremists.

In alcohol use, for example, Finns are rather extreme. Those, however, who are not extreme users, tend to be extremely non-using. The Finnish word for "temperance" is *raittius*; the term for "total abstinence" is *ehdoton raittius*. Finnish "temperance societies" throughout Finnish communities of the United States tolerated no drinking and should have been called "abstinence societies." One of the problems is that Finns don't realize alcohol should be drunk more slowly than buttermilk.

Keeping the Faith

Theology has been filtered through the personalities of Simon Peter, John, and Paul. It has been percolated through Finnish personality traits as well. Let me give a few examples.

Grandpa (Vaari) Lehto was a man who enjoyed his children and grandchildren and patiently put up with the minor problems that came with kids. One day, as a daughter was visiting with her very young child, the youngster threw a first-rate tantrum. With no obvious provocation, the little tyke lay on the floor kicking and screaming. Vaari Lehto kept rocking in his rocker and observed, "I can't believe there are some folks who don't acknowledge original sin!"

After a year of graduate theological study in Finland, my friend Dr. Walter Kukkonen was ready for a call to serve in the Finnish Evangelical Lutheran Church in America (the Suomi Synod). He duly received and accepted a call to serve the congregation in Kaleva, Michigan.

He, of course, had not known that the Board of Directors of Suomi College and Theological Seminary (now Finlandia University) was about to issue him a call to teach at the seminary. Nor had the Suomi Board of Directors been aware of the call process at Kaleva.

The Suomi board did issue its call right after Kukkonen had accepted the Kaleva call. The situation presented a dilemma for the pastor. However, since he felt God had led him to pursue graduate study for years in hopes of eventually teaching at a theological school, Kukkonen resigned from Kaleva and accepted the call to Suomi.

The situation presented a dilemma for the congregation as well. One of the council members wondered whether Kukkonen really knew God's will: "Would God change His mind like that?

Are you sure He wanted you to come here in the first place?"

Unabashed, Kukkonen answered, "I knew He wanted me to come. I just didn't have any idea of how long He wanted me to stay!"

A church council member remarked in disappointment, "Until now, I've at least believed in God and pastors, but now I guess I don't believe in pastors anymore."

Kukkonen responded, "Well, perhaps that is why God sent me here. Put your faith only in God."

The most interesting incident related to Kukkonen's brief tenure at Kaleva happened at Lake City, a preaching station where Kaleva's pastor conducted services on the last Sunday of each month. He preached his *tulosaarna* (initial sermon) and at its conclusion tendered his resignation! Following the service, there was a welcoming coffee hour, with the presentation of a purse to the new pastor. The prepared remarks of the congregation representative had to be revised a bit to accommodate the situation.

Folks have noticed that many of my stories are from pastors. It is only natural that those who deal closely with lots of people can see how absurd we human beings, with our sins and self-righteousness, must look to our Creator since we often look silly even to each other.

Just as Simon Peter was identified by a particular accent, so today various disciples of Christ speak with characteristic accents. We have listened to some of the uniqueness with which Finnish Lutherans speak of their Master. It is important that our accents not deny our Lord but witness to Him and serve His flock.

In fact, since His Father was father of all nations, Jesus had some Finnish characteristics. The following are only three illustrations of why some folks think Jesus was at least partly Finnish:
- He went into the wilderness for forty days.
- He was a great fisherman.
- He was into washing people clean—even their feet!

Sauna Bathing

This section is, in a way, a summary of the Finnish characteristics we've noted, because the sauna reveals the extreme thoroughness, toughness, and naturalness of the Finnish approach. And, of course, the cleanliness! For Finns, personal cleanliness has to be at least skin deep, and that's where the sauna comes in. Coming clean was especially important at the beginning of life; in the days before neonatal units in hospitals, what place was a cleaner setting for birth? Thus, many Finns were born in a sauna. Preparing for special occasions, such as the Sabbath, Christmas, or one's wedding, sauna was a "must." Finally, when life ended, the body was washed in the sauna as preparation for the funeral service and burial.

The sauna is a Finnish development of an ancient European bath culture. It is an interesting Finnish East-West hybrid, somewhere between the dry Roman bath and the wet Turkish steam room. Finns have clearly put their stamp on the sauna and have made it their national pastime. In fact, Finland has been referred to as the "land of sauna, *sisu,* and Sibelius." Finns are passionate about their saunas. They can't always get to a hot spring, but the hot spring of the sauna can be in the house. It's good to remember that, even though Finns have a good deal of technological know-how, they still stay with some primitively satisfying interests.

Since Finns are currently noted for their creativity, and since creativity supposedly results from 10 percent inspiration and 90 percent perspiration, it may be that Finns have benefitted much from going to the sauna!

The very word "sauna," which refers both to the bath and to the bathhouse, illustrates a characteristic of the Finnish language. In Finnish, there isn't any playing of games as to what should be pronounced how. Finns don't say "sawna"—they pronounce *every* letter, including the "u": sauna!

Some of you readers don't remember way back when we had mere typewriters instead of word processor keyboards, but I can tell you that one of the early exercises in Typewriting 101 was "How now, brown cow?" I suggest that saying "How now, brown sauna?" will help us pronounce the word correctly. On a Tom Snyder TV program, actress Christine Lahti made a point of the correct pronunciation of "sauna" and recounted how she and her siblings rolled in the snow after sauna in Michigan. She has a sauna in her home in California even now.

How about playing "Twenty Questions" about the *kiuas* (the rock-filled stove)? Well, it's mineral. Yes, it's bigger than a bread-box—at least twice as big! What's a "sauna cocktail?" Just water on the rocks!

Beyond the words, there's the harsh reality of the experience. The sauna is not for sissies! Saunas are more than just a lot of hot air (the Roman pattern), which can dry out the lungs and nasal passages! There has to be a modest amount of humidity (about 15 percent), which is created by throwing water from ladles or cups onto the heater (*kiuas*). That air is still much drier than that of Turkish steam baths and allows for the sauna's high temperatures (175°–205°), which facilitate perspiration. The sauna is something one gets used to by degrees—170, 180, 200 degrees!

Saunas are becoming well-known and loved around the world, becoming increased imports in China, for example. Sadly, in some areas they, like massage parlors, are misused as coverups for prostitution. (Now there's an oxymoron for you: "coverup for prostitution!") For Finns, who believe that one should behave in the sauna as in church, that is a crime!

We who are between the Earth's molten core and the burn of the Sun depend on fire. But we tend to forget that, and we need the sauna, which can re-ignite imagination and passion. In the sauna, one has a kind of liturgy of *löyly* (vapor). There is nothing put on about a person who is naked, without pretensions, coming clean through self-flagellation with birch whisks and bathing. In the midst of our rush-rush life, many turn to meditation, yoga, tai chi, or other organized helps for relaxation. For Finns, the sauna provides relaxation of muscles from hard labor or exercise, peace for the mind from the constant noise of our culture, and a spirit at ease with oneself, other people, and the world at large.

Finnish sayings have gathered the essence of the sauna experience:

Ihminen ilman saunaa on kuin ruumis ilman sielua. (A person without sauna is like a body without a soul.)

Emännätön talo on kuin löylytön sauna! (A house without a wife is like a sauna without heat!)

Sauna on köyhän miehen apteekki. (The sauna is the poor man's pharmacy.)

Hikinen päivä, sanoo Mäenpään faari, kun oli saunapäivä. (Old man Maenpaa said, "It's a sweaty day," because he was going to sauna.)

Hullu kylöpöö, jotta nahka palaa! (A person's crazy if he takes sauna until his skin burns!)

One might say to someone who is blushing: "You're blushing like the backside of a sauna bather."

Conclusion

The top 10 factors which make folks Finnish are:

10 a hunger for rice pudding,
 9 love of lakes,
 8 search for mystery in forests,
 7 enthusiasm for sports,
 6 response to music,
 5 the *Kalevala* and other poetry,
 4 *sisu,*
 3 sauna,
 2 the Finnish language,
 1 great genes.

MY GRANDFATHER'S WATCH

At this hour of night, I must wind
down, call it a day. But after toothbrush
and pajamas, before benediction
and bed, I must wind some things up—
two old-fashioned watches.

In this era of digital timepieces,
I turn to pieces of other times—
times of longer work-weeks,
shorter lives, and yet, perhaps, more
time to savor the gift of life.
I like the way my old watches tell
time—through faces and hands,
rather than by digits and blips.

I wind my faithful Hamilton wristwatch,
bought in Hancock, Michigan,
in '49, a transition time of my life.
The inner workings have been repaired,
the face has been cleaned, the brown
leather strap replaced a number of times.

And I wind my grandfather's Hampton,
the only thing of his that I own
except, of course, for some genes.
Jaakko Hillilä's nickel-cased, sturdy
pocket watch was bought in 1880,
carried to work in Oscoda, Michigan.

My grandfather's watch is just right
for my shelf. It did not stop
short, when the old man died.
Without heirs, Reino, another grandson
of Jaakko, wanted me, my son Marty,
grandson Nate, and any subsequent
"Hillilas" to watch over this watch.

I look at the time, see the watch has
gained, so I must re-set it. I pull out
the small lever near number V and set
the time to 12:30—tomorrow already!

Comments on
Finnish Americans

Ethnicity is difficult to define. The definitions even of "race" are imprecise. In 1890, in the U.S. census, "mulatto" was defined as 4/8–5/8 Black. Subsequently, even quadroons (1/4 Black) and octoroons (1/8 Black) have been considered Black, although they are predominantly white. Recently, Americans have had difficulty understanding Tiger Woods' ethnicity. He's 1/4 Vietnamese, 1/4 Chinese, 1/8 white, 1/8 Indian, and 1/4 African American. Most Americans just think of him as "Black!"

The edges of any ethnic identity are smudged. Consider U.S. census statistics. In the first place, ethnicity is defined by self-identification. There is no allowance made for fractional nationalities, even when the father is known. "Hispanic" is an invention of the U.S. Census Bureau.

What should all of us Americans do? We have received complex patterns of genes, which give us some uniqueness but also much to share. We are in this Americanism together with lots of other good folks. But if we are to give coming generations a clear idea of our American uniqueness, we should identify and rejoice in America's diverse heritage of people with various backgrounds. Thus we can avoid becoming ugly Americans.

Each of us stands between the dead and the unborn. Since cloning is not yet an option, we shall pass on our genes always together with someone else's genes. Even if we have no children, we pass on our examples and teachings.

To give our children wings, we first let them see their roots. We are conduits, splices, hinges, joints between our ancestors and our descendants. We change from being descendants to becoming ancestors! We may know who a few of our forefathers were, but we have no idea of who our descendants will be a hundred years from now. Whatever we are, we pass on. What we are is shaped not only by the genes that are locked within us but by the environment around us and the choices we have made to become our unique selves.

In our current ethnic mix, what should Finnish Americans do? Each Finn has received genes—Finnish and non-Finnish genes. (Remember: Finns, too, go back to Adam!) What can our Finnishness mean as part of a unique, God-given endowment? Like most Americans aware of their roots, Finnish Americans can enjoy being transcultural.

American Finns can develop a sense of the glory of immigration.

If we succumb to the appeal of homogeneity, we continue life under an alias. Finns are part of the diversity that we celebrate in the United States. A native American Indian told President Clinton: "Be careful with your immigration laws. We weren't, and look what happened!" Seriously, often the brightest and best from many lands have come to the United States as immigrants. Nearly half of the Finnish diaspora live in the United States. Second is Sweden, with Canada third.

Soon after the Daughters of the American Revolution had refused to let African-American Marian Anderson sing for them, Franklin Delano Roosevelt addressed their assembly: "Fellow immigrants," rubbing in the fact that even descendants of *Mayflower* arrivals and the president of the United States were all of immigrant stock, just as Marian Anderson was!

I mentioned to someone that I was of Finnish "descent." He kidded me, "That figures, because I guess you have to 'descend' pretty low to be Finnish." I explained that the term just means we're genetically of Finnish stock, and we're really pretty high up on the human ladder. Seriously, it's good for us Finns to know more about our roots and ourselves, to think of who we are. With Finnish *sisu,* I have kept in touch with my heritage, including proficiency in the language. It amazes me that the former United States Secretary of State, Madeleine Albright, did not know her parents were Jewish although she had lived with them!

I don't want to be considered a "professional Finn," but I certainly cringe at the casual erasure of ethnic origins. Many Europeans have knowledge of their ancestors for many generations. In contrast, most Americans can't name their eight great-grandparents. I can't immediately name mine. Can you?

There are natural reasons for our ethnic amnesia in America. We are descendants of people who have left the old countries. Many children of immigrants to the United States never saw their grandparents, who were left in the "fatherland." The ocean kept to a minimum any contact with ancestral areas. Americans therefore generally have much less sense of who they are ethnically than do Europeans.

Sometimes erasure of ethnic origins has been a consistent pattern imposed on a group, the most noticeable instance being the canceling of African-American heredity. Black slave families and ethnic groups were separated, so that their Ethiopian or Nigerian or other national languages and ethnic identities were systematically destroyed. Their only ethnic identity has become Black.

In other instances, ethnic groups tried to make themselves invisible so that they and their children would be considered true, assimilated Americans. Often the third generation tried hard to remember what the second generation had tried to forget. The first generation still had an identity, a foreign identity of aliens in a new land. The second generation was between identities, a "marginal generation," no longer fully identified with the old country, not yet fully integrated into the new. The third generation developed an American identity.

Members of immigrant communities are often uncertain of their identities, particularly members of the marginal generation between the immigrant generation and the Americanized generation. Immigrant Finns at times became obsessed with the question: "What do *they* (the more Americanized and more fluent in English) think of *us* (the more recent arrivals)?" There were conflicts regarding which traditions should be discarded, which preserved, which reconstructed. Whatever the direction of assimilation into American culture, Finnish Americans kept their faith in education and hard work.

Finnishness has not left a very legible mark on the map of the United States. Except for their share in the Swedish immigration to Delaware in the 1600s, Finns were latecomers to the New World. Thus, the United States has a New England and a New Mexico but no New Finland. There is a Finland in Minnesota—a community of a couple of hundred residents. (You can get to it by taking Route 61 either from Duluth or from Thunder Bay, Canada, to Route 1, then going about five miles west, toward Ely.)

Our country has appropriated various European capitals, such as Paris, Berlin, London, Venice, and Athens, but no Helsinki or Turku. There are even New York and New Orleans, but no New Helsinki or New Karstula in our land. We do have some Finnish touches, but mostly in villages: Suomi, Kaleva, Tapiola, Nisula, Elo, Oulu, Toivola, Wainola, Makinen.

It is important to note that Finns tend to preserve their ethnic identity more than many other national groups. There are several reasons for this. First, I suspect that some Finnish traits we have noted, like shyness and *sisu,* are operative.

Furthermore, Finnish immigration to the United States was later than that of Swedish or German groups, for example. Finns did not arrive in America on the *Mayflower.* They were later immigrants, probably coming over on some "Novemberflower"!

A certain Finn had planned for a long time to leave Finland for America. He was scheduled to get on a boat at Hanko on Wednesday morning. Fearing he was late, he ran to the pier and saw a boat just leaving. Even though it was about six feet away, he ran while holding his suitcase above his head, jumped and just made it. A puzzled crewman said, "What's your hurry? This boat is coming in!"

Of the 2,227 passengers on the ill-fated maiden voyage of the *Titanic* in 1912, at least sixty-three were from Finland, twenty of them survivors. In the 1940s, in Brooklyn, New York, we knew one of them as "Titanikan Tilta"—Mathilda Backström, who had been born in 1879!

It is also clear that we Finns are more unique genetically and linguistically than many other ethnic groups. When Finns came to America, the aborigines they found were English-speaking Irish! Finns are clearly set apart—for better or for worse.

Swedes and Norwegians share many factors: Their genes have given similar appearances, their languages are similar, and their cultural patterns have much in common. When pressed to explain the difference between Swedes and Norse, a Swede will ponder a moment and then say, "Well, the Norwegians have better neighbors!" A Norwegian will give a reverse response.

Finns, however, are Scandinavians only because of history and proximity. When Finland was part of Sweden from 1209 to 1819, it was logical that Finns could be called Scandinavians. However, Finland was part of Russia from 1819 to 1914, and the world knows Finns aren't Russians! Finns said: "We are not Swedes; we aren't going to become Russians; let us therefore be Finns!" In the Upper Peninsula of Michigan, Finns learned they weren't Irish or Italian.

Finnish Americans are doubly enriched because they have the blessings of two cultures. Of course, that may mean that a second- or third-generation Finnish American has been less thoroughly immersed in the current American culture. For example, in "Who Wants to be a Millionaire" most participants come from the current American cultural background. Someone who came from a dual Finnish-American background would be handicapped because much of what they've learned about *Kalevala* and Finnish language, hymns, sports figures, and so on, would never show up in the contest questions. Learning that information has meant not being exposed to some aspect of American culture.

Finns have had to live with more ambiguity than many others. That is why there were Red Finns and White Finns. That is why it was so difficult for some Finnish-American fathers to see their sons go off to World War II, which placed the United States on the side of Russia.

A century ago, Finns came to the United States as immigrants, eager to begin a new phase of life. Now, Finnish corporations are coming to America, often through acquisitions of American companies. They are making their presence known from Atlanta to Berkeley, and from Texas to Minnesota.

American Finns can take pride in legitimate achievements.

Esko built his house with a pine tree off each corner, some junipers on either side of them. Foundation plantings, he knew, were good to tie the new house into the existing lawn and community. But he left some areas where the foundation would show—he was proud of it.

Finnish Americans are developing a sense of pride for legitimate achievements, which are numerous. I've even been told that the fellow who started Finns Anonymous has disbanded the organization and joined Finlandia Foundation!

What are some of the areas in which Finnish Americans have made notable contributions?

Education

Hannu Heinilä of Finland has conducted research regarding Finnish immigrants who pursued higher education at three American institutions: Suomi College/Finlandia University, Valparaiso University, and the University of Minnesota.

Finns in America established Suomi College and Theological Seminary in Hancock, Michigan, in 1896. The theological seminary is now part of the Lutheran School of Theology in Chicago, formed by the mergers of German, Swedish, Danish, and Finnish Lutheran theological schools. Suomi College is now Finlandia University, continuing in Hancock as a representative of Finnish culture and language. It is a degree-granting institution of higher education, currently including in its offerings a design program in cooperation with institutions in Finland.

A surprising number of Finnish immigrants turned to Valparaiso University in Valparaiso, Indiana, for higher education. During the fifteen years before World War I, two hundred fifty students with Finnish names were enrolled at Valparaiso. Assuming that an equal number of Finns with non-Finnish names were enrolled during that time period, the yearly average is over thirty. Those were the Brown-Kinsey years, during which Valparaiso was recognized as "the poor man's Harvard," and was a national leader in higher education. In 1907, Valparaiso University was second to Harvard in student numbers, with an enrollment of 5,000 in fields from penmanship to medicine. Students enrolled in the medical or dental programs spent two years on the Valparaiso campus, the rest in Chicago. Dr. Talso, our family doctor in Ishpeming, Michigan, was a Valparaiso University Medical School alumnus. The Valparaiso medical school tradition now continues in Chicago as part of Loyola University.

Religion

I remember a Finnish immigrant recounting what his mother advised as he left home: *"Kun menet sinne Atlannin taa, pidä se Raamattu repun päällä, eikä sen pohjassa!"* ("When you go across that Atlantic, keep the Bible at the top, not the bottom, of your sack!")

Since there is no state church in the United States, Finnish Lutherans here have divided into several groups. Regardless of divisions, there were some constants: coffee, for example. I don't remember any Finnish churches smelling of incense—it was coffee and cardamom *pulla!* Lutherans of other ethnic backgrounds sometimes reproached Finnish-American pastors of making coffee the third sacrament!

The Finnish Evangelical Lutheran Church in America (Suomi Synod) was established as the daughter church of the Evangelical Lutheran Church of Finland. In 1962, it merged with the United Lutheran Church in America (of German background), the Augustana Lutheran Church (of Swedish background), and the American Evangelical Lutheran Church (of Danish background) to form the Lutheran Church in America. In 1988, that church body joined with the American Lutheran Church (formed in 1960 of German, Norwegian, and Danish church bodies) and the Association of Evangelical Lutheran Churches (formerly part of the Lutheran Church-Missouri Synod) to form the Evangelical Lutheran Church in America.

Finnish immigrants rooted in the Evangelical Revival of Finland founded the Finnish National Church, which has affiliated with the Lutheran Church-Missouri Synod. Finnish immigrants related to the Laestadian Revival—referred to by some as "those Finnish Amish!"—formed the Finnish Apostolic Lutheran Church, which vigorously maintains its separate identity.

It is only natural that with mergers of seminaries and church bodies, many Finnish-American Lutherans may feel they are becoming an endangered species. However, tradition is best preserved not as a separately pickled product but as an ingredient contributed to a larger whole.

Not all Finns are religious, of course. There was a history of resistance to religion already in Finland. Consider Lalli, who murdered Henry, who had come as a missionary to heathen Finns.

In addition to those who may be against religion, there are Finns, of course, who, like members of all other nationalities, have simply become indifferent—have lost their religious heritage. However, even those Finns who have opted against faith in God and participation in the Church are heirs to the language and literacy developed in that heritage. I remember hearing of the atheist parents in Iowa who argued for the teaching of religion in public schools because they "wanted their children to know what they don't believe." The Christian faith is part of our Finnish heritage. Compared to Croatia or Northern Ireland, Finland has a unified religious heritage.

Cultural Organizations

Someone has said, "There are three kinds of people: those who can count and those who can't." He improved on the fellow who said, "There are two kinds of people: those who say there are two kinds of people, and those who don't." Well, when I grew up, there were two kinds of Finns: church Finns and hall Finns. Some of the halls were temperance halls or Kaleva Society halls; others, however, had a leftist agenda committed to a socialism.

Seriously, in spiritual commitments as well as in size and personality, there are *all* kinds of Finns. Like all humans, they have sought beyond body and mind to spirit. They have not all gotten to God, but most of them have gotten at least to cleanliness, which they believe is next to godliness. Since all human nature abhors a vacuum, and since we all need some kind of belief system, some Finns have been thorough in their commitment for religion, others in their zeal against it. I think God, who asks us to be hot or cold rather than lukewarm, must appreciate Finns.

In Brooklyn, New York, Yrjö Johnson was an interesting example of divisions among Finnish Americans. For much of his life, George had been committed to the communist ideology, but in the forties, he felt betrayed when he saw what the Soviets did to Finland. He came to me, then pastor of Gloria Dei Lutheran Church, and very forthrightly said, "I think I've been on the wrong path. I'd like to join the Church and return to the teachings of my childhood." He was welcome, of course, and became a member and regular attendee. He joined the church choir, singing out heartily with his resonant bass voice. Once, when someone said at a Finnish choir practice, "Let's sing *'Oi, Herra, luoksein jää'* ('Abide with Me')—everyone knows that!" George countered, "Hey, we never sang that at the Communist Hall. How does it go?" He once volunteered to sing a solo at the informal midweek service. He sang the melodious bass part to *"Oi, Herra, luoksein jää"*!

The appeal of communism led some Finns to embrace atheism. After one of my lectures at FinnFest USA in Minot, North Dakota, a lady came to me and said sweetly, "I'm one of those atheist Finns. I'm glad you at least mentioned us." I said, "I respect your choices, but it's never too late to make better ones." Both of us chuckled, and I hope she has thought more about it.

The Finnish spirit has also been advanced by diverse Finnish cultural organizations. Echoing the Finnish national epic, the Knights and Ladies of Kaleva have been devoted to Finnish culture. Workers' halls and temperance societies promoted the Finnish spirit through programs, theatre, and musical productions. Additional significant contributions have been made by FinnFest USA, the Finlandia Foundation, the Finnish American Translators Association, and Salolampi Finnish Language Village. The Finnish spirit in America is also nurtured by the Finland Society (Suomi Seura), which is headquartered in Helsinki.

Although the Finnish contribution was weakened by division into "church Finn" and "hall Finn" groups, increased cooperation has been achieved recently. It is also encouraging that Finns on both sides of the United States/Canada border cooperate in a number of matters. In the year 2000, FinnFest was a joint celebration by Finns of the United States and Canada.

The Printed Word

A number of newspapers and journals were founded for a literate group: *Työmies, Eteenpäin, Raivaaja, Amerikan Suometar, Minnesotan Uutiset, Amerikan Uutiset, Auttaja, Lasten Lehti, Paimen Sanomat.* Yearbooks were also issued by religious and secular organizations. Recently, English-language journals have appeared: *Finnish American Reporter, Nordic Way, New World Finn, Finnish Update.* In addition, the *Journal of Finnish Studies*, published by the Finnish Studies Program, University of Toronto, and edited by Börje Vähämäki, edifies readers of both the United States and Canada.

American Finns can pass on what they have received.

America generally is becoming increasingly diverse. A few years ago, I participated in "Being Ethnic, Being American: A Regional Conversation," sponsored by the Indiana Humanities Council. It is clear that the face of America is changing and will change more in the years ahead. Europeans constituted 90 percent of immigrants a century ago. Now, non-Europeans make up 90 percent; in 1951–1960, 52 percent of immigrants came from Europe. In 1981–1990, while 10 percent of U.S. immigrants were

European, Asians grew from 6 to 38 percent.

How long does an ethnic identity last in a diverse new land? Ole Rolvaag worried: "Soon we will have reached the perfect democracy of barrenness. . . . Dead will be the hidden life of the heart which is nourished by tradition, the idioms of language, and our attitude to life. It is out of these elements that character grows."

We have a constant dialectic of the past with the future going on within us. I don't know much about genealogy, except that I've been called the sap of my family tree! I respect those who give much time to tracing their ancestry, but I am mostly interested in progeny. We can, of course, get nourishment from our roots, but we can't change them—they are given. I am more concerned about the twigs that will grow into branches and bear fruit.

Recently, quite a few members of our family went to Finland to explore our roots. But we rejoiced more in what we experienced of branches: our present-day clan members, Finland's current future-oriented people, culture, arts, sports, and churches.

Poet laureate Pinsky wrote in *Bostonia,* Winter 1994–95:

"I'd been thinking about the word 'matrix' and wondering whether it was related to the word 'mother.' And I'd been thinking a lot about the immensity of the past behind any given moment. That is, it's not that I have just two parents who made me. I was made by four grandparents, eight great-grandparents, sixteen great-great-grandparents. And if you go back a couple centuries, by thousands and thousands of people. . . . Almost anything you can think of probably happened among one's ancestors. Of course, everyone is descended from a king. Of course, everyone is descended from someone who starved to death, or who was a beggar. Everyone is descended from a prostitute. Everyone is the result of a rape somewhere back in history. And indeed, we are all brothers and sisters if you look back far enough."

There were people of ill repute even in Jesus' lineage, as the Gospel according to Matthew reminds us.

A recent Pickles cartoon echoed some of the Pinsky comments about multiple forebears. Grandpa was telling his little grandkid: "A lot of people are counting on you." "Like who?" "Two parents, four grandparents, eight great-grandparents, and so on: one million forty-eight thousand five hundred and seventy-six people all involved in the creation of *you*. Don't let us down!" "Geez! Peer pressure is nothing compared to ancestor pressure!"

I would revise that grandpa's message. I would hope that the expectations of our descendants are weightier than the expectations of our forebears. There are millions of persons coming after us. They have a right to expect from us: clean air, a healthy environment, unspoiled natural treasures of forests and oceans, examples of strong morals, a legacy of good values.

Each of us has a rich and varied genealogy. However, at this point, we should worry more about our progeny. In a train, I like to face where we're going rather than where we've been. I am like the waist of an hourglass—through me pass the generations of the past, through me are channeled genes and values for the future. It is that future for which we value our traditions.

What are some of the values American Finns have received? For starters, Finns have shown a remarkable cooperative spirit, which could lead some to communism but which could also be a blessing as a counterweight to dog-eat-dog competition and too-rugged individualism. The spirit shown by the Amish in their barn-raisings and by Habitat for Humanity was also evidenced in Finnish communities through the cooperative movement, with its stores and apartment buildings. A community spirit has often led to *talkoot,* community projects in which all pitch in and help. For a number of years, our family lived in a cooperative apartment in Brooklyn. We did shopping at the *Osuuskauppa* (Co-op Store). The rebuilding of Gloria Dei

Church in Brooklyn, after a devastating fire, was an inspiring example of volunteers cooperating for a common cause.

Although most Finnish workers' organizations and co-ops have been dissolved, there are a number of organizations through which American Finns can cooperate, such as the Finlandia Foundation, church congregations, hall organizations, music and dance groups. Cooperation is furthered by Finnish-American newspapers and strengthened by FinnFests and numerous area festivals.

If Finnishness is to survive, perhaps it needs new emphases. Project 34 seeks to involve Finnish Americans of generations three and four. I fit right in with that project—my grandparents all came to the United States as immigrants, which makes me a third-generation Finnish American. In fact, I've suggested that we work on "Project 345," since my grandchildren, fifth-generation Finnish Americans, are much interested in things Finnish.

The Finnish language is not essential for Finnishness. According to the 1990 U.S. census, 660,000 citizens claimed Finnish as their "ancestry or ethnic origin." However, only fifty thousand of them (fewer than one in thirteen) claimed that they still spoke Finnish at home. Although American Finns maintain their ancestral language proficiency more than many other ethnic groups, the rate is still less than 8 percent!

More and more Finnish-American societies, churches, and clubs are functioning in English. Decades ago, many churches of Finnish background in the United States lost members because they were too slow in adopting English as a second language for worship. Sons and daughters of Finns who married non-Finns left those Finnish churches in which their spouses could not worship meaningfully. In some cases, insistence on continuing use of Finnish in church worship has been counterproductive.

Most Finnish-American churches have merged with churches of other backgrounds and have contributed a Finnish presence within larger congregations. A few congregations continue to have a distinctively Finnish flavor—for example, Zion Lutheran in Fairport Harbor, Ohio, and St. Andrew's in Lake Worth, Florida. Surprisingly, a few congregations have recently appeared, which obviously strive to cater to recently arrived Finns serving people related to the Finnish consulate, as in New York, or Finnish corporations, as in Atlanta and Dallas.

Paavo Kortekangas, retired Bishop of the Tampere Diocese, has been actively involved with Finnish Americans, especially in Florida. He asked why some American Finns still wanted church services in the Finnish language, even though they had lived in America for decades and spoke English on their jobs and even in church before and after services. One fellow answered: "Don't you understand that I learned to pray to God in Finnish. My God speaks Finnish!" I, too, feel a nostalgia while singing Finnish hymns, reading the Finnish Bible, and listening to a Finnish sermon. However, it would probably be better if everyone worshiped God in the language of their daily conversations. The Reformation encouraged people to use the vernacular language.

Many American Finns are limited to English. More important than fluency in the language is an appreciation of the culture. A person who lacks *suomenkieli* (Finnish language) may have *Suomen mieli* (Finnish empathy).

Some Finland Finns manage nicely with Swedish, as did Finnish-American philanthropist Thor Soderholm, at whose wedding I officiated in Brooklyn, New York.

Aune Shilongo, a Namibian woman, knew both the Finnish language and Finnish spirit. That petite, Black woman, who had learned Finnish from missionaries to Namibia, knocked on our door in Valparaiso, Indiana, one afternoon and asked, *"Puhutaanko tässä talossa suomea?"* ("Is Finnish spoken here?") She enjoyed our basement sauna, and she loved to sing Finnish hymns. That's the Finnish spirit!

If a person has the opportunity to learn the Finnish language, that language can be enlightening and rewarding. It is gratifying to know that among the language villages sponsored by Concordia College in Moorhead, Minnesota, is Salolampi, the Finnish Language Village.

American Finns can
keep the Finnish flavor.

The Bible refers to an "instrument of ten strings," which has kinship with *santir*, dulcimer, harp, and the Finnish kantele. In his *Guide to Small Kanteles*, Gerry Henkel writes: "I will tell you about the kantele. The kantele is a Finnish box full of music. Actually, the box does not contain the music; that is in our souls. This Finnish box is just a simple tool to move music out of our souls and into the world."

From personal experience, I can report that the kantele is also a user-friendly musical instrument. After dinner in a Finnish home, I sat down at the sofa and began picking at a kantele, which was lying on a coffee table. Plucking a few melodies by ear, I was doing Kreeta Haapasalo's *"Mun kanteleeni kauniiimmin taivaassa kerran soi"* ("In heaven my kantele will sound more beautifully"), when I noticed the hostess laughing. When I inquired whether she shouldn't be feeling devotional instead, she answered, "I suppose your kantele will sound better up there in heaven, because down here you're playing that thing upside down!"

I deferred to authority, of course. However, at a recent Suomi Conference festival, I noticed that one of the kantele players played her instrument with the narrower side toward her, whereas the other two played theirs with the longer side toward them. I pressed Melvin Kangas, the program leader: "Which is the correct way to play the kantele?" He answered: "Either way!" No flute or French horn would be as accommodating!

All ethnic groups in America bring their recipes from across the seas. Many Finnish Americans still relish Finnish foods: rice pudding, fruit soup, *pulla, viili, rieska,* milk potatoes, and lingonberies. A video, *Traditional Finnish Recipes that Bridge the Generations,* focuses on the Finnish accent in cooking. A Finn won't "turn up" a nose at a turnip or even a rutabaga—he'll make a delicious mashed and baked casserole out of it. Personally, I wish *sillisalaatti* (herring salad), *uunijuusto* (rubber cheese), *kalja* (Finnish near beer), and prune tarts were more available in American cuisine! Oh, and *korppukahvit* (coffee with oven-baked cinnamon toast to dunk)!

If one adds raisins or craisins with a bit of honey to *rieska* (Finnish flatbread), the result is something reminiscent of English scones.

During the Depression, we used to eat the roe *(mätiä)* of bass, pike, and other fish, that Dad and I caught. Fried along with the fish, it was delicious! Fish eggs—wouldn't that count as "caviar"?

There is no doubt that, in coffee drinking, Finnish Americans are trying to boost the American average of less than two cups per person per day toward Finland's record 4.9 cups!

Finnish flavor is evident even in home furnishings. I'm remembering a lady who said that she couldn't bring much from her home in Finland to this new country, but she did bring her most significant weavings, paintings and prints, which made the rented apartment seem like home in spite of the foreign setting.

American Finns can join in the joy of festivals.

St. Urho's Day (March 16)
Recently, the observance of St. Urho's Day has received much attention in parts of the United States. While it may come as a surprise to residents of Utah and Hawaii, March 16 has now been recognized, at least on paper, as St. Urho's Day in all fifty states!

In 1956, Richard L. Mattson, then a manager at Ketola's Department Store in Virginia, Minnesota, submitted the "Ode to Saint Urho," which was published in the local newspaper. That same year, a St. Urho's Day celebration was held in St. Paul, orchestrated by the late Sulo Havumaki, then professor of psychology at Bemidji State College. Those two men articulated a myth which had been an oral tradition in the Finnish community. The myth tells of an invented saint who chased the grasshoppers out of Finland to save the vineyards. (According to Matti Kaups, in *Finnish Americana,* the grasshopper eradicated by the fictional saint is known as *Locustidae Finnicus bastardus.)* Currently, there are many St. Urho's Day parades, a "St. Urho Polka," paintings, plus countless St. Urho T-shirts and novelty items. There are two Minnesota statues of St. Urho: one in Finland and one in Menahga. A photo of the Finland statue adorns the cover of my earlier book, *FinnFun*—Urho's the better looking of the two fellows pictured.

As a visiting pastor, I was once giving a children's sermon as the church year was moving from the post-Easter season to the Sundays after Pentecost. Since the linens on the altar and pulpit and the stole on the pastor had changed color, I thought it would be instructive to talk about the meaning of those changes. I put stoles of various colors on the altar rail and began to explain how the white expressed the joy of Easter. A lad quickly helped me out: "And the green is for St. Patrick's Day!" A Finn kid chimed in right away, "And the purple is for St. Urho's Day!" Well, I had some explaining to do after that. I'm sure the congregation remembers what the kids said better than what I said.

By the way, how about appointing an "Urho of the Year" at St. Urho's Day festivals?

Midsummer Day (St. John's Day—June 24)

This date, six months from Christmas, is a holy day in the Christian calendar, marking the birthday of St. John the Baptist. It is also celebrated as a secular Midsummer's Day, with bonfires, singing, and dancing.

FinnFest USA (usually in July)

Of all Finnish-American festivals, it is clear that FinnFest USA is the tops. FinnFest lasts for several days, typically beginning on a Thursday afternoon and closing on Sunday afternoon. These celebrations have been held in Michigan and Minnesota, of course, but also in California, Oregon, Washington, North Dakota, Illinois, Florida, Delaware, Massachusetts, and Maine. In the Millennial Year 2000, Toronto, Canada, was the site of a joint United States/Canada Finn Grand Fest.

Hosts for the Minot, North Dakota, celebration were accustomed to hosting large ethnic festivals, some, like the Norse Fest, drawing as many as sixty thousand people. FinnFest, however, was different, they said: "You Finns are so academic. There are so many lectures and workshops going on, not just concerts, dancing, and crafts!"

FinnFests are also done with homegrown talent. Local committees are often amateurs doing a once-in-a-lifetime thing. Performers are from the Finnish community. (I noticed that Bill Cosby was one of the feature attractions for the Norse Fest, and I doubt whether he's Norwegian!)

Christmas

Finns in this country observe Christmas with a passion. In the Suomi Synod, Christmas services in Finnish were at 6:00 a.m. Once, I had difficulty with that since the English midnight service had ended after 1:00 a.m. Esther and I lived in a parsonage adjoining the church, and we woke to the organ music preceding the early service! I quickly put on my pants, clergy shirt, and collar over my pajamas and went to the sacristy, where I added my clergy robe. I entered the chancel just in time for the first part of the liturgy!

A few years ago, Nilla Järvinen, whom we had gotten to know when she was an exchange student from Finland at Valparaiso High School, visited the Adneys (her "American parents") and us at Christmastime. One evening she came over and said, "It won't seem like Christmas unless I can sing some Finnish Christmas hymns!" So the three of us stood in our living room and raised our voices in many hymns, including the traditional *Hoosianna.*

In addition to the religious observation, of course, there are Finnish dimensions to our eating at Christmastime. Together with other Nordic peoples, we claim to enjoy lutefisk *(lipeäkala),* which has been defined as "the piece of cod that passeth understanding." By the way, note the honesty of the Finnish term: literally, "lye fish."

Other Festivals

Finnish-American festivals have been held regularly in countless communities throughout the United States. In many communities, Finnish Independence Day and *Kalevala* Day are observed. In addition, many Finnish organizations celebrate with annual festivals.

At this writing, Finlandia Foundation has the following chapters: Baltimore, Maryland; Boston, Massachusetts; Colorado; Florida; Inland Northwest and Seattle in Washington; Los Angeles, Long Beach, Palo Alto/Stanford, and Santa Barbara in California; National Capital; Houston and Dallas/Fort Worth, Texas; New York Metropolitan; Pittsburgh, Pennsylvania; Tidewater, Virginia; Twin Cities, Minnesota; Chicago, Illinois; and Portland, Oregon.

Knights and Ladies of Kaleva lodges are found from east to west. Finnish Heritage Societies exist in South Paris, Maine; Canterbury, Connecticut; Fitchburg, Massachusetts; and Ashtabula County, Ohio.

Monson, Maine, boasts a Finnish Farmers' Club it founded in 1935. Two temperance societies remain: Uljas Koitto in Quincy and Sovittaja in Rutland, Vermont. The Aura Seura in Voluntown, Connecticut has celebrated its seventy-fifth anniversary. Festival Finlandia is observed in August at Ironworld, near Chisholm, Minnesota. Naselle, Washington, holds a Finnish-American Folk Festival in July. Finlandia Days are observed annually at Bryant Park in Lake Worth, Florida. Finnishness is alive and well in Palo, Minnesota, where an annual *laskiainen* festival draws great crowds. Finnish-American Societies are also found in Vermont; Warren, Maine; Cape Cod, Massachusetts; and Tucson, Arizona.

By the way, since many Finnish festivals now include boot-throwing and wife-carrying, I regularly take along two pieces of sports equipment—a boot and my wife!

And, of course, American Finns can share the sauna.

The first Finnish saunas in America were made entirely of natural materials—no metal, just a wooden building with a heater built of stones. The sauna was used for bathing, of course, but also for birthing, massage, bloodletting, and preparing the body for burial. There, fish and meat were smoked. Typically, the homesteader first built a sauna, in which the family lived while it built the house. Non-Finnish neighbors sometimes suspected that Finns were about witchcraft in the strange sauna buildings. Gradually, however, they began to like sauna bathing themselves. According to the Estonian ethnic historian Matti Kaups, there were over 250 public saunas in Minnesota's Finnish communities during the 1920s and 1930s.

Dr. Andrew Weil of Arizona University, who has received much attention on the cover of *Time* magazine and elsewhere for his holistic, integrated approach to health, is a staunch advocate of the sauna. In *Eight Weeks to Optimum Health,* he recommends starting with a sauna once a week in Week Five, increasing it to twice a week in Week Six, and being in a health-promoting, well-established habit of sauna three times a week by the end of the eight-week program. Dr. Weil promotes the sauna at the end of the eight-week program:

> "In Week Five, I asked you to experiment with sweat bathing in a sauna or steam room. . . . If you like it, I recommend it as an ongoing addition to your lifestyle at whatever frequency is convenient. Perhaps you have located a facility you can use at a nearby health or fitness club or a friend's house. . . . You might consider installing a sauna . . . in your own home. When I moved to a new house three years ago, I had an old closet converted to a steam room that my wife and I use regularly."

Dr. Weil's enthusiasm for the sauna is based on several factors. First of all, sweating is good for us, because it allows the body to rid itself of unwanted materials, such as minerals, drugs, and toxins, decreasing the workloads of the liver and kidneys. Furthermore, it is relaxing and spiritually refreshing. Weil says, "In asking you to take up the practice of sweat bathing, I cannot separate its physical and spiritual aspects." Finns put it more picturesquely: *On lämmin ja lysti, kun napakin savuaa!* (It's so warm and such fun, that smoke even comes out of your belly button!)

During a sabbatical semester some years ago, I went to Finland to study Uno Cygnaeus, the father of Finland's school system. (Horace Mann is the Uno Cygnaeus of the United States.) The day before returning to the States, I passed a sauna shop in Helsinki. I went in and bought two sauna *vihtas* (birch whisks for self-flaggelation). I believe in the old saying "A sauna without a *vihta* is like a meal without salt." When I got to customs at O'Hare, I realized I was in trouble. The customs agent looked at those leafy things in the plastic bags and asked what *those* were. "Well, sir, I'm Finnish, and we Finns go to a hot bath, where we beat our naked bodies with these things to aid perspiration and stir up the blood circulation. I'm returning from Finland and thought I'd like to bring a couple of genuine Finnish *vihtas*." He wasn't going to fall for a strange line like that, so he called his superior and said, "Here's a strange one for you!" (I think he meant the customs problem.) So I started again, "Well, sir, I'm Finnish. . . ." He rolled his eyes a bit and said, "Just a moment, I'll call the supervisor." He came back with a huge Black man, who asked, "What are you trying to bring through customs?" I thought it wouldn't be any use explaining Finnish ways to him, but Finns are persistent so I said, "Well, sir, I'm Finnish. . . ." At the end of my spiel, he held up a *vihta*, pretended to beat himself on the back with it, grinned broadly, and said, "Yeah, I know. Go ahead. Enjoy!"

An ideal location for a sauna is on a lakeshore. I grew up in Upper Michigan, and I still remember fondly the summer cottage our family had on the shore of Fish Lake. It is an experience of physical and spiritual peace to go from a steam room into a fresh lake, then back again into the sauna, and eventually to sit on a bench outside the sauna drinking something cool and looking at the restful beauty of nature. There's no difficulty finding a lake in Finland—it is the land of one hundred thousand lakes.

At Finnish celebrations, such as FinnFests or Lake Worth's Finlandia Days, saunas have been featured attractions.

Conclusion

As Finnish Americans have participated more and more in American society, they have discovered that they are not from the shallow end of the gene pool. They have registered major achievements. Of course, different people value different things. For example, one day I heard two kids bragging. One said, "My big brother can punch in his computer and get on the Internet to all kinds of cool things and send e-mail even to Germany!" The other retorted, "Yeah, well, my grandpa is Finnish, and he can take his teeth right out of his mouth and put them in a glass!"

GRANDFATHER EINO

Mäntyjärvi—just one of Finland's 100,000 lakes—
embraces each of its dozen islands. It washes
the clean beach—and the granite beside the beach.

Beside the lake, a modest sauna of pine logs
smokes its last pipe for that midsummer Saturday,
sends mini-clouds rising toward the high sky.
Through thin soil, the sauna's posts rest on granite.

Beside the sauna, a birch grows pine-high
toward a sky flying Finland's colors. In its bark,
it bears the names of Sulo and Onni, lads who left
it long ago. Its roots cling stubbornly to clefts
in the granite base just below the skin of the soil.

Grandfather Eino sits on a bench at the foot
of the birch beside the sauna and contemplates
the lake, smokes one last pipe for the day,
thinking of Sally, Tommy, Tiffany and Dan—
his grandchildren who grow in America.
The old soldier's heart is not granite. . . .

SULO (A Rondelet)

Deep furrowed lines
crease Sulo's brow, drawn there by genes—
    deep furrowed lines
etched deeper still by grief's designs
and farmer's work since early teens.
Fields still are Sulo's favorite scenes—
    deep furrowed lines.

Catalog of
Comparative Cultures

Since many Finnish Americans visit Finland and many Finland
Finns come as tourists to the United States, it may be helpful to
note some of the differences found in the two societies. I believe
that Finland and the United States both have interesting mixes of
the practical and the impractical. The differences noted below are
not in the spirit of faultfinding or putting down procedures of
either country, but, rather, to show that some procedures can be
done in more than one way. I have presumed to commend each
country for some customs.

Advantage: Finland

On the basis of my limited travels in Finland, I have listed some
customs in which I think Finland has the edge:

- addresses in which the street name comes before the house
  number, the zip code before the town;
- dates in the order of day/month/year, instead of putting the
  day between the month and the year;
- elimination of "a.m." and "p.m." by using all 24 hours of
  the day for travel and concert schedules;
- use of 20s for both coins and bills, whereas Americans use
  20s for bills, 25s for coins;
- prices usually listed in even marks (euros now, I suppose)
  rather than an American-style $7.99;
- restaurant bills which include taxes and tips;
- simple auto license plates without pictures, advertising or
  slogans;
- granite curbs;
- troughs carved across sidewalks for rain to run from down-
  spouts to gutters;
- highway signs to remind drivers to "keep distance" between
  cars, with markers both on the pavement and at the road-
  sides to indicate the proper distance;

- frequent, convenient blisters (additional paved shoulders) for bus stops along the highways;
- public transportation easily available (possibly because gasoline usually costs over $1 per liter, about $4 per gallon);
- bikes—lots of bikes, and many bike paths;
- hotel rooms with hot pipe racks for drying towels, all water faucets coded red for hot and blue for cold, and inflatable clothes hangers;
- light switches set low, so kids can reach them;
- toilets that flush easily with a pull-up knob at the top of the tank;
- church steeples as separate campaniles rather than being built on the tops of church roofs;
- church pews with slanted tops to hold hymnals.

Ah, there's more

Instead of a parking meter for every parking space, there are centrally located meters in Senate Square, which take coins (on our last visit, 1-Fmk, 2-Fmk, 5-Fmk and 10-Fmk coins, but euros now, I suppose) and give a printout of the time of the transaction, the length of parking time that is bought, plus the expiration time. The slip is placed inside the windshield to give evidence that the vehicle is legitimately parked. I once saw a tourist go up to the meter, put in five coins, taking the printout after each coin, thus getting five proofs that he could park for the next 12 minutes! I'm sure he thought he was getting an hour's worth of parking. I wasn't about to spoil his fun because I knew that a Finnish meter maid would surely accept his explanation.

A few years ago, one transaction at the post office amazed me. I had books related to research on Uno Cygnaeus and wanted to send them to the United States for further reference. I took them to the post office; there a clerk eyeballed them, found a suitably sized box, wrapped and addressed them!

There are some creative Finnish touches. For example, each table in outdoor restaurants seems to have upside-down flower pots in large ashtrays—smokers tap ashes and toss their butts into the little holes in the flower-pot bottoms, so the wind won't blow cigarette litter around. Well, they don't toss *their* butts—just the cigarette butts—into those pots!

Advantage: USA

I commend the United States for the following procedures:

Since American cities are so young compared to many in Europe, they tend to have wider, straighter streets, making for easier driving.

Because of the language differences, road signs in America are simpler for the eye to understand, for example, MERGE rather than *OHITUSKAISTA LOPPUU.* Also, because of more conspicuous location and only one language, street signs seem more driver-friendly in the United States.

The United States seems to be leading the way in providing handicapped-accessible facilities—even subway stations and cathedrals. At a Hesburger (hamburger joint) in Helsinki, I went down twenty-two narrow steps to a basement WC!

American restaurants provide more nonsmoking sections. Also, diet drinks are more readily available, as are decaffeinated coffee and soft drinks. By the way, do you remember the cow that had an abortion? They called her "De-Calf"!

In communicating, the area code plus seven-digit telephone numbers of the U.S. are simpler for some of us numerically challenged!

We have noted some practical things about bathrooms in

Finland, but America has more convenient shower areas, especially in hotels. Those areas are not just curtained off from the rest of the bathroom but are set in tubs so that no water spills over the floor. And even though Finland is the cleanest country on earth, American bathrooms provide more washcloths!

Furthermore, water is more readily available in American restaurants. And ice is more abundant in ice machines and water glasses, even in Florida, than in arctic-climed Finland.

The foregoing differences between Finnish and American customs are not black or white—often they are just a matter of degree. Besides, I haven't been in Finland for a few years; things may have changed!

Just different
There are many customs and procedures that are neither better nor worse in Finland than in America—they're simply *different*.

The Finnish calendar week often begins with Monday rather than Sunday, with weeks listed vertically instead of horizontally on wall calendars.

Instead of declaring a weekday holiday for Election Day, Finns vote on the more convenient of two consecutive days—Sunday or Monday.

Minor religious festival days, such as Epiphany, Ascension Day, and St. John's Day, are observed on the nearest Saturday rather than on the numerical day specified by the religious calendar.

Generally, name days are celebrated more than birthdays. (By the way, the Finnish name "Eino" is literally a "No-no" for bilingual American Finns!)

In the late 1980s, Finns decided Valentine's Day was a nice touch, so they began to celebrate it but gave it a different, less romantic spin—Friendship Day.

Finland can disorient a person with the 5:00 p.m. summer sun still shining at 10:00 p.m. Even if one stays up all night, that's not very long! Ah, but in the winter, one gets the darkness back with a vengeance!

In Finnish the decimal point becomes a comma; the comma after the first number in 1,000 becomes a space. Since the number 1 is written to look somewhat like a 7, the 7 needs a line through it—7. Also, where we say "seven-thirty," forward-looking Finns say "half-eight" *(puoli kahdeksan)*.

The speed limit signs look great at first—120! Then we realize: the number is in kilometers per hour, about 75 mph. Also, driving lanes are usually merged out from the center lane, rather than into it.

Finland uses DC instead of AC for electrical current, Centigrade instead of Fahrenheit for temperature.

Hotels regularly have floor 13 and room 13. (Perhaps Finns are less superstitious than Americans!) Bed making is different, too, with the top sheet and blanket folded into a package.

In Finland, one sees signs reading *OTTO* on the sides of buildings. I suppose English-speakers pronounce it "Auto," which is O.K., because *Otto* indicates an *auto*matic teller machine—ATM. The Finnish *otto* means "take," as in "Come for your take from this machine!" Finns named Otto have gotten a new twist to their name.

Finnish vending machines seem to be more versatile. In one of the hotels, I once saw a Vendco machine that offered candy, cigarettes, dental needs, cigars, and pantyhose!

There are no equivalents of American drugstores; there are pharmacies, of course, and kiosks which sell cosmetic and other convenience items. In America, we have Kmarts. I thought perhaps Kmart had merged with the Ku Klux Klan in Finland, because we saw many KKKK-Marts!

Vertical siding is popular on many wooden buildings in Finland.

Ads fill the front pages, instead of interior pages, of newspapers.

Baseball has been modified to *pesäpallo*; the pitcher becomes a *syöttäjä* (feeder) just lobbing the ball; the runners go clockwise instead of counterclockwise. Soccer, of course, is bigger than American football. In schoolyards and on playing fields, one can see athletes doing triple jumps and throwing the javelin; in the U.S., those sports are generally limited to collegiate track teams.

Moose are called elk in Finland. What if you belonged to the Milwaukee Moose Lodge and when you visited Finland, you were called an Elk? Well, elk is fine for culinary matters. During our 1997 visit, we had a delicious repast of elk and *lakka* (cloudberries) at the home of relatives.

Among delicious foods we found in restaurants were carrot, pineapple and radish salad, and a *kaalipata* (cabbage casserole of chopped cabbage, ground beef, and carrots). *Kotipizza* (home pizza) was popular among pizza parlors. Perhaps the most unique souvenir we brought home was some *viili* (Finnish yogurt) starter, which provided many bowls of *viiliä*.

For breakfast, in addition to coffee and milk, we were offered buttermilk. Instead of fried or scrambled eggs with sausage or bacon, we usually ate salami, cheese, and hard-boiled eggs.

There is little skim milk in Finland but quite a bit of *acetofilus*, a stomach-friendly milk variety. In restaurants, one can order a large or small coffee served in small or large cups. Pear soda and pineapple soda are included among soft drinks.

Whereas Americans are continually shifting their utensils while eating, Finns keep forks consistently in the left hand. There are very large spoons (for porridge) and very small spoons (for coffee) but fewer regular-sized teaspoons.

It should be emphasized that many of the "different-from-America" items are not unique to Finland but rather are part of the differences between America and Europe in general. One of the benefits of traveling is the realization that something may be done differently than "our way." An "ugly American" abroad assumes all other ways are wrong; the thoughtful traveler learns to appreciate other points of view, other practices. I have a theory that *ugly* Americans are those Americans who are so far from their foreign roots that they have become arrogant!

ON A ROLL
*Studies in Finland have shown
that one pat of Benecol three
times a day helps promote
healthful cholesterol.*

One Pat Benecol,
bless his soul,
was jammed on a bun
with sweet cherry jelly,
headed for Mäkinen's
cholesterol belly.
He said, to be droll,
"Cherry, *Ma chérie,*
we're on a roll!"

Essay on the Finnish Language

In the midst of the world's Babel, let's invent a perfect language. It should be phonetic, of course. Just one sound for each letter. Just one kind of sound for each consonant. Just one length of sound for each vowel. But instead of its being an artificial language, like Esperanto, let's have real live people speak it. Well, we have it—it's Finnish!

Finnish is not a Scandinavian language; it is Finno-Ugric. Languages of the Finno-Ugric family are spoken by about twenty-three million people. Of those languages, however, only three —Finnish, Estonian, and Hungarian—seem to have a future. Estonian has close kinship to Finnish, but that language is spoken by even fewer people; Hungarian is but a shirttail relative to Finnish. The rest are vulnerable minority tongues within the Russian Federation. Within the Baltic-Finnic language group, Karelian, Vepsian, Ludian, and Votian plus Ingrian dialects are spoken only in Russia. Even though Karelia is a republic within the Russian Federation, only 10 percent of its people speak Karelian; some Karelian speakers live outside Karelia, in the Kver region.

Finnish is spoken by only 0.06 percent of the world's humans. Therefore, it's no wonder that the reaction of some folks is: "Yes, I'd like to learn a foreign language, but not *that* foreign!" In his memoirs of being a correspondent in Moscow, Walter Cronkite refers to the Cronkites' Finnish cook who had difficulty with both Russian and English and, therefore, "spoke no known language."

Mikael Agricola (circa 1510–57) created standard, literary Finnish. A skillful linguist and educator, he served as the Bishop of Turku, but is best known as the creator of the *Aapinen* (Finnish ABC Book) and Catechism and translator of the New

Testament into Finnish. Agricola had to assure Finns that their heritage was compatible with the Christian message, and that God could understand even their language! April 9 is observed as Agricola Day in Finland.

All living languages constantly change. If you doubt this, just try to understand some teen-age jargon! In his "Introduction" to the book *Valinkauhassa (In the Melting-Pot),* my father apologized for the impoverished Finnish he and other second-generation American Finns used in their speaking and writing because they were so "far from the fresh springs of the Finnish language." I, of course, am two generations beyond the language he used.

We won't be able to seal the Finnish language hermetically. If a language is static, it's dead! Cultures are portable, fashions merge, cuisines fraternize. (Perhaps Finnish rutabaga casserole will conquer the United States!) Humanity is a "melding" pot of languages (yes, the languages "meld" or merge, rather than "melting" down); the languages beg, borrow, steal from others. Let's just say that languages share. We must face the fact that Finnish, like all living languages, is losing and gaining its voice.

Linguistic Characteristics

To begin with, let's admit that Finnish looks like a tough language. When Greeks can't read something, they don't say, "That's Greek to me!" They say, "That's Finnish to me!"

When people look at printed or written Finnish, one of the first reactions is, "Boy, it has lots of long words!" However, Finnish isn't as complicated as it looks. The length of this agglutinative language is due to compounding, running words together. For example, "nuclear material tests" becomes *ydinainekokeet. Aseleponeuvottelutoimikunnansihteeristö* is actually "the secretariat for the peace negotiations committee." Some believe Finnish words should be uncompounded, broken up into their component parts. Finns, however, for a long time have expressed frugality by running their words together. That saves the space bar and an estimated three pages of reading in an average novel.

Finnish words indicating things usually end in vowels: *uuni* (stove), *talo* (house), *sauna* (sauna), and so on; words describing activity can often end in consonants: *menen* (I go), *olet* (you are), etc. As in English, concrete things are often expressed by short words: *kivi* (stone), *ase* (weapon), etc.; words expressing abstract concepts usually are longer: *hengellinen* (spiritual), *yleinen* (general), and so forth.

In some ways, Finnish simplifies language: Who needs articles? Also, why not toss prepositions and do their work through case endings? English allows for this in a limited way, allowing either "of the country" or "the country's." Finnish really allows for it and ends with fifteen cases!

However, it has been noted that creativity is in the prepositions, which change relationships. If true newness is desired, it can be reached better by changing expectations (using prepositions) than by adding another item (using nouns) or adding another action (using verbs). How then can Finns still be so creative if their language has zero prepositions? Oh, it's in the suffixes, which function as prepositions!

An area of Finnish consistency is in verbs. In most languages, verbs are generally conjugated in a regular way—I think, you think, he thinks, etc. The verb "to be," however, is quite irregular in most languages—I am, you are, he is; *Ich bin, du bist, er ist, wir sein, und so weiter;* or *Je suis, tu es, nous sommes, ainsi du reste.* Finnish is an exception, with greater regularity from *olla* to *olen, olet, on, olemme, olette, ovat.*

For those who like unisex approaches, Finnish should be appealing—there is no gender. Feminists in Finland have had a rough time because of this factor. For example, no one can be accused of making God masculine by using the pronoun "He"— *Hän* is neutral, inclusive!

One aspect of Finnish that I like very much is its rather peaceful nature. Violent English has us "kill time;" Finns just waste time *(haaskaa aikaa).* Finnish swearing is not into sexual violence, whereas many English speakers seem obsessed with the f-word. Finns instead take out their anger more properly on a wealth of terms for devil and hell!

Finnish is an exceptionally poetic language, mellifluous in sound and full of similes and metaphors.

Pronunciation

First of all, Finnish is "articulated" mostly at the front of the mouth rather than "swallowed," thus more easily understood when spoken or sung than many other languages.

Furthermore, the accent in Finnish is *always* on the first syllable, with a secondary accent on the third. This is hard for English speakers to master: "Hel´sin-ki" becomes "Hel-sink´i," because English typically accents the second syllable of a word. "No´ki-a" becomes "No-ki´a" because folks assume it's Japanese and should be pronounced like English.

Since Finnish words are *always* accented on the first syllable, Finns are inclined to say "To´ron-to" rather than "To-ron´to." In Negaunee, Michigan, Antonio Guizetti, the owner of a music store, gave up trying to get Finns to pronounce his name "Guizet´ti"—not "Gu´zetti," which in Finnish means "had to empty his bladder!"

Daughter Christine is a psychologist and often is asked to testify as a witness in court proceedings. She uses her difficult Finnish maiden name professionally, which is the reason for the following exchange recorded in a transcript of a court proceeding.

Attorney: Dr. Hil´li-la, you again testified that you had been seeing this family for approximately two-and-a-half years; is that correct?

Witness: Correct.

Judge to witness Hillila: Excuse me, just a minute. You don't mind if your name is made mincemeat of, do you?

Witness: I am used to it.

Attorney: Am I mispronouncing it?

Judge: It took me a long time to learn how to pronounce this name, so I am very sensitive to it. It's Hil-lil´a.

Attorney: Hil-lil´a. Am I right?

Judge: Hil-lil´a?

Witness: Sorry, Your Honor, but I swore to tell the truth—Hil´li-la.

Judge: Is the accent on the first syllable?

Witness: It is, it is.

Judge: Hil´li-la. Okay. I stand corrected.

Attorney: Thank you, Your Honor.

Finnish is also wonderfully phonetic. Why have a language in which there is a question how words are spelled or pronounced? Who would ever guess that a word spelled "h-e-a-d-a-c-h-e" would be pronounced "hedeik?" Before English lessons, what Finn could believe that "c-o-l-o-n-e-l" and "k-e-r-n-e-l" are both pronounced the same? Or that "ri-mem´bör" is spelled with three "e's"!

English has 1,120 different ways of spelling its forty phonemes, the sounds which are needed to pronounce all English words. In contrast, Finnish phonemes are always spelled the same way! One result is that dyslexia, which affects 15 percent of Americans, is less than half as prevalent in Finland. Most adults, with 15 minutes of instruction, can read Finnish aloud with correct pronunciation! Finnish dictionaries need no pronunciation guide after each word. The Finnish law-abiding, rules-following nature carries over to the language. There is one drawback to a phonetic language: it eliminates spelling bees. What you pronounce is what you spell!

Various languages have unique pronunciations. For example, some languages begin words with *sr, phth, drz* or *vrsk,* which are strange to English. The only troublesome pronunciations for English speakers learning Finnish are the vowel "y" and the consonants "k," "p" and "t."

Finnish has a mellifluous sound, because it has a wealth of

vowels, and the consonants are soft. The unique aspect of the consonants "k," "p" and "t" is that they are not exploded unless they are doubled, as in *ukko, akka, nappi, hattu.* The pronunciation of a single *k* is halfway between the English "g" and "k;" the *p* between the English "b" and "p;" the *t* between the English "d" and "t."

The Finnish *j* is pronounced like the "y" in "yes," or the way it is pronounced in German—*Jawohl, Jungkind,* etc. Americans make it equivalent to the "g" in "genius, Genesis," etc. That can cause huge problems. For example, the Jass (pronounced "Yass") family from Denmark came to the U.S. and named their son Hugh, not knowing how Americans would pronounce Hugh Jass.

I am reminded of the elementary school student who was learning about human anatomy: "The body consists of three parts—the *branium,* the *borax,* and the *abominable* cavity. The branium contains the brain; the borax contains the heart and lungs; the abominable cavity contains the bowels, and there are five of them: a, e, i, o, and u." Well, Finnish has eight bowels: a, e, i, o, u, y, ä, ö!

The Finnish *a* is pronounced as the "a" in "alone;" the Finnish *e* like the "e" in "get;" the Finnish *i* as the "i" in "sin;" the Finnish *o* like the "o" in "allocate;" the Finnish *u* as the "oo" in "cook;" the Finnish *ä* ("a" with umlaut) like the first "a" in "canary;" the Finnish *ö* like the "o" in "word," except that it's short; the Finnish *y* is a vowel similar to the German *ü* and the French *u,* midway between "i" and "u"! Wherever one encounters a single Finnish vowel, it is pronounced short; two short vowels make a long one! And there are lots of vowel movements in Finnish: double vowels and diphthong combinations of vowels. Combinations of Finnish vowels—the diphthongs such as *eu, ui, uo, yi, yö, äi, äy, öi, öy*—can be problems for the novice linguist: Try to find even a slant rhyme in English for *löyly* or *ryijy!*

H. Armstrong has given helpful hints for pronouncing Finnish:

> *b, c, f, w, x, z* do not exist in Finnish; pronounce very
>   quietly.
>
> *r*   rolled strongly; false teeth an advantage.
>
> *h*   clear your throat lustily; that's it.
>
> *uu* as in the Arabic.
>
> *äy* half palatial, half alveolar, half dental; scornful
>   expression.
>
> *yö* be very careful with this.
>
> *yi* never as in "Hi-y-yippy-yippy-yi."

I can add these:

> *öö* the most common vowel sound in English, as in "bird" or
>   "Byrd," "curd," "furred," "heard," "nerd," "slurred,"
>   "word."
>
> *ää* imitation of a sheep.

One reason why Finnish looks foreign to American eyes is the use of umlauts. Consider a sign we saw on a Helsinki trolley: *"24.7 Uusi Pizzahut Töölössä!" (Töölössä* has four umlauts in eight letters!) English gets by with six vowels, because it allows a vowel to be pronounced in more than one way. Check the "a" in "cat," "date," and "alms." By using umlauts, Finnish is able to assign just one sound to each vowel.

Many of you know that some computers don't send umlauts in e-mail. The omission of umlauts can cause serious trouble, however. For example, perhaps the e-mail uses *passi* (passport) instead of *pässi* (ram), and so on. As a result, there currently are many creative ways to indicate umlauts in e-mail.

The sound of a special word is often significant. I had a pious friend who would utter, when completely flabbergasted: *"Perunoita saatavana!"* It sounded innocuous enough ("Potatoes available!"), but other Finns knew he was thinking *"Perhana! Saatana!"* ("Devil! Satan!"). The sweet benefit of Social Security is commonly referred to as *sosiaali sokeri* (Society's Sugar).

Finns don't have the worst problems with English. For example, since someone knocked the "l" out of the Japanese alphabet, our Japanese friends have generally substituted "r" for "l" in speaking English. That has caused all kinds of confusion. That made my name Hirrira. Worse yet, the election problems in Florida became "erection" problems!

Since Finnish is thoroughly phonetic, there are *no* silent letters. Phonetic language words sound fairly similar whether they're read forwards or backwards: Toyota (Atoyot), sauna (anuas), Hillila (Alillih). In non-phonetic languages, words often sound completely different when they are read backwards:

    hay—yah
    weight—thgiew
    storage—egarots
    center—retnec

Since Finnish is a phonetic language, punning is rare. Thus, Finns have been fascinated by the possibilities of English. When Aino was criticized for changing her mind, she responded: "Tat vas 'yes'-terday; today a 'not'-erday!"

Names

Once, while I was in Finland, I wondered why my speaking was heard as non-native. I realized that instead of pronouncing my given name in Finnish—Bernhardi—I was pronouncing it "Bernhard," which would have been spelled "Pöörnhard." And they knew there was no name like that!

No rational person would call for language to be as pure as Ivory soap. I don't insist on an umlaut in Hillilä, because to most Americans umlauts are either a bother to bring up on the computer's character map or an affectation as in Häagen Dazs.

However, the general linguistic feel of a language through accent should be maintained. Le-pis′to doesn't sound as nice to me as Le′pis-to! I asked Anttila why he gave his name as An-til′la. He said it sounded less foreign, and besides, he didn't want to be "anti" anything. I suggested to him that it would sound better to be known as Ant′ti-la the Finn rather than An-til′la the Hun!

Consider some of the interesting sounds of Finnish names: Saara Leivo from Sarajevo, for example. A Finnish-American kid named Pentti was very cooperative, never sassed; in fact, Karhu, his father, thought he might become a cellist, because he was always saying, *"Joo, joo, Ma!"* ("Yes, yes, Mom!"). When Uuno went to Mexico, he was "Numero Uno," of course! Lily told her husband Ensti that she was planning on joining the church's Women's Guild; Ensti told his friends that she was "lilying the guild!" Even though his name was a double-negative, Eino couldn't say "No" in either language, and he got into big trouble! I had always hoped to introduce Oliver Hallberg at some festival, announcing: "And now for the Grand Finn Ollie!" After Liisa Raisio had worked for a while for a real estate company, she began to specialize in condo sales and rentals, becoming known as "Condo Liisa Rais!" And then there was the guy who was happy he married a "Kolehmainen's daughter."

My father-in-law's name was Armas, but since that seemed strange to non-Finns, he became known as Harvey. And his wife, naturally, was "Harvey-nainen" (exceptional)! Her given name was Impi, but she was not impish! Vaara, often spelled Waara, is a rather common family name, meaning "wooded hill," possibly from the location of a house; the word also can mean "danger." Since the Halttunen home was on a wooded hill, and his wife's name was Impi, Armas called his place Impivaara, which can mean either "the nymph's wooded hill" or "Danger: Impi!"

Mantila gave a sizable gift to Finlandia University in honor of his deceased in-laws. Maybe it was conscience money because he hadn't treated them too well while they were living. He thought it would be nice to have the gift in his wife Anu's name. Come to think of it, maybe he still didn't want to be too closely associated with Anu's folks. In any case he gave it in Anu's name *(Anun nimes)*. When he didn't see her name listed among donors, he inquired about the oversight. A college official responded, "Didn't you say the gift was 'Anonymous'?"

A colleague chuckled as he told me that one of his children confessed: "You know, when you talked about 'Auntie Lepisto,' I thought you were speaking about some maiden aunt in the family, not about Pastor Antti Lepisto, the president of the Suomi Conference!"

The Stierna family in Ashtabula, near Jefferson, Ohio, was known for giving their children unusual names. Pastor David Hartman was performing a baptism for a daughter who was to be named Eufrosyne Günther. One of the congregation members didn't catch the name and asked the lady next to her: *"Mitä se pappi sanoi?"* ("What did the pastor say?") *"Eihän se muuta, kuin että Jeffersoniss' kynnetään!"* ("He just said that they're plowing in Jefferson!")

Someone at the CNN financial news desk had to explain to Saku Katajamaa that Fred Katayama was not originally Katajamaa—he's Japanese! And someone told me that the original Bond in the 007 movies was Pantti. He must have been kidding!

The February/March 1997 *LFAS* [League of Finnish American Societies] *Newsletter* listed the following tongue-in-cheek examples of Finno-nyms and how they may be interpreted by non-Finns:

Aalto = singer
Ivari = piano key

Jokela = comedian
Kamppinen = outdoorsman
Kiltinen = Scottish dress
Wuori = fret
Tikkanen = clock
Manninen = male
Rautio = AM-FM
Wirtanen = viral bump

Difficult Finnish names don't necessarily kill success. The world's fourth-largest consulting firm is Pöyry, which is into construction, and environmental and energy consulting.

You probably heard why Raappana was offered a job at the Michigan Bureau of Motor Vehicles. He was told, "We need someone who knows Finnish. We've been getting complaints from Houghton County objecting to some of the license plates we've approved. We thought words like *PERKELE* (DEVIL) and *PIERU* (FLATULENCE) were proper names!"

Sometimes proper names become complicated when combined. Helvi Rinta married Taisto Liivi. They were both strong supporters of gender equality, but they couldn't become Helvi Rinta-Liivi and Taisto Rinta-Liivi, the equivalent in English of "Mr. and Mrs. Brassiere." The reference to strong supporters reminds me of the high school principal who was known as a "strong athletic supporter."

Also, regional dialects create deviations: Elma becomes "Elmer" in New England, and Elmer, as compensation, becomes "Elma." I sense some gender confusion or cross-addressing there! Even stranger: After Toivo had a sex-change operation, she was called Hope, which is a direct translation!

Names in all languages can have interesting aspects. In our area,

"Smith" makes concrete. I asked Cruikshank, who made our television case, "You don't have a crooked shank, do you?" He answered honestly, "No, but one of my ancestors did, and we're stuck with that as a name!" The name of Tony Lima, the movie director, doesn't sound very tony to Finnish ears; since "Lima" is spelled with only one "i," Finns pronounce it "Lima" meaning "slime." On the other hand, some non-Finnish names could adapt well to Finnish: I suppose Sgt. Bilko could become Kersaantti Ilkka, and Elvis could segue to Ilves.

Place names also can cause misunderstandings. A Finn settling in Florida asked, "Why do you pronounce it 'Lan-ta'na' instead of 'Lan'ta-na'?" He was told that the "lan'ta" accent would remind people of manure. He wasn't about to give up his Finnish accent and proclaimed, *Lantana se on ja Lantana pysyy!*" ("It's manure, and it'll *stay* manure!") I'm sure it was a "manurity" opinion.

Losing Something in Translation

To be a good translator, one has to have a two-track mind. Or maybe three-track since the translation is a *tertium quid* between the two languages. Robert Frost said it well: "Poetry is what gets lost in translation."

For example, a Frenchman was trying to explain his situation: "My wife, you see, is unbearable. Ah, I mean she's impregnable. Ah, I mean she's inconceivable. What I really mean is that she can't have babies!"

A few examples of Chinese mistranslated to English: "Please leave your values at the front desk." (Sign in Shanghai hotel elevator.) "Please drop your trousers here" (at a Wuxi drycleaner). "Order your summer suits quick. Because of big rush, we will execute customers in strict rotation" (outside Tianjin clothing shop). "Ladies may have a fit upstairs" (in a Xian tailor shop).

The Finnish *kyyhkynen* can be translated as either "pigeon" or "dove," but there is quite a difference of image, whether the Scriptural wording is: "A dove rested on Jesus" or "A pigeon roosted on his head."

Translation boo-boos have been labeled *käännöskukkasia* (translation blooms) in Finnish. Here are a few remarks prompted by recent mistranslations from English to Finnish: "Butterfly" is not *voikärpänen* (lit. butter fly)! "Delight" doesn't mean to put someone's lights out! A "tank top" is not the gasoline tank cover—in fact, one isn't supposed to "top off" when the tank is filled! And a "workout" is not yard work.

There are mistranslations from Finnish to English as well. A cute waitress in Kaleva Kahvila (Kaleva Coffee Shop) was asked by a flirtatious male customer: *"Saanko sumpin?"* ("May I have a kiss?") The waitress asked another waitress who was more fluent in Finnish: "What does that guy want in his coffee?"

Since *home* means "mold" in Finnish, a recent immigrant read "homeless person" as *"home*less" and translated it: "A not moldy person!"

Elaine Lillback of Painesville, Ohio, reported: "When I first visited Finland, I thought it must be a really boozing nation, as every shop had a sign 'ALE' in the window. After a while, my Finnish kicked in and I realized it was 'short' for SALE—*ale* for *alennus!*" So, if you see an ALE sign in Finland, translate it as "sale," not "ale!"

KELIRIKKO (lit. weather damage) is a sign often seen on the roadway to warn of frost heaves. When we toured Finland with Dr. and Mrs. Raymond Luomanen back in 1955, Mrs. Luomanen, a nice Polish-American girl, at one point looked at her map puzzled: "Kelirikko? Weren't we in that town already earlier?" You could say she committed a *kielirikko* (lit. language damage) or fractured the language.

Translation can have surprises. For example, "American football" is known as *Jenkkifutis* (Yankee footsie) in Finnish. A musical "sharp" becomes a *risti* (cross). Having a "bone to pick" or "something in his craw" translates to something *hampaankolossa* (lit. in the cavity of a tooth). "Flapping one's gums" becomes *huulenheitto* (lit. throwing one's lip). "Ostrobothnia" (lit. east of the Sea of Bothnia) becomes *Pohjanmaa* (lit. Northern land).

A "harebell" (lit. "rabbit bell") is translated *kissankello* (cat's bell). To be more consistent, call it by its other name, "bluebell," because in Finnish it retains the blueness and the bellness by being *sinikello*.

One would think that "buttercup" might be translated *voikukka*, but that's "dandelion," which originally was French, *dent-de-lion*, or "lion's tooth!" If you do see a "buttercup" in Finland, it's a *leinikki!*

"To be a ventriloquist" is literally "to speak from the stomach" (L. *venter+loqui*). The Finns come right out and say *vatsastapuhuminen* (speaking from the stomach), but in English, we hide behind Latin.

How does one refer to "sex" in Finnish? Well, it can be rendered *seksi*, which sounds like Finglish. Or it can be rendered *sukupuoli* (lit. sex-side), but that just sounds like "gender." Or try *sukupuolielämä* (lit. sex life), but that seems to take the life out of sex.

Victor Borge made quite a splash with his "inflated English," through which "wonderful" became "twoderful," "appreciate" became "apprecinine," and so on. He had trouble when he tried to translate the concept into Finnish. What kind of response does one get elevating *yksitoikkonen* to *kaksitoikkonen*, inflating *viisumi* to *kuusumi*, stretching *kuusisto* to *seitsemänstö?* Well, I guess the Nelimarkka family might appreciate becoming at least Viisimarkka!

Sometimes, translation can kick it up a notch. For example, "a bit of good fortune" becomes *onnenpotkaus* (lit. "a kick of fortune") in Finnish. A fishing "fly" becomes more elegant: *perho* (butterfly). "Pike perch" (lit. *haukiahven*) sounds like fishy miscegenation, so Finns give it a breed of its own: *kuha*. "Tightrope walker" becomes *langallatanssija* (lit. dancer on a string); "line dancer" is something else again. "Brassiere" in Finnish becomes *rintaliivi* (lit. breast vest), which makes more sense than "brassiere," which derives from the French *bras*, which means "arm" and seems to be misplaced! Also, rather than yelling the strange term "Fore!" when golfing, Finns are quite clear: *Pallo tulee!* ("The ball is coming!") *Laulu vaikeinta* (lit. hardest task is singing) and *kissanpäivät* (the days of a cat) both speak of one who leads the life of Riley—how's that for a case of "Finagled Finnish?" "Carpal tunnel syndrome" sometimes caused by over-use of the computer mouse becomes *hiirikäsi* (lit. mouse-hand)! "Chairperson" or "chair" becomes a more logical *Puheenjohtaja* (conversation director)—after all, the chairperson is probably the only one *not* in a chair! (The French logically use *le Président*—"the presider.")

Sometimes linguistic borrowings make one wonder whether it's really translation, as in *Pekka Pikka poimi peckin pippuri picklesiä* for "Peter Piper picked a peck of pickled peppers." Perhaps it's early Finglish! McDonald's rye hamburgers in Finland have become *McRuis!*

Some translations are just interesting. An *ABC Book* is known as an *Aapinen!* A "gizmo" is a *vehkain.* "Sic 'em!" becomes *puskii!* If you "snore" in Finnish, you keep the onomatopoeia: *kuorsaa.* A "ladies' man" is *naisiin menevä mies* (lit. a man who gets into women)—think about it. I've never heard of a gay man characterized as *miehiin menevä* (a man who gets into men)! *Ikälikkö* (lit. age-flaunter) is a name for "codger" from the Savo district.

Polttaa pilviä (lit. burns clouds) means "smokes marijuana!" *Päissään* (lit. in his heads) refers to someone who is drunk. *Miestä vahvempaa* (lit. stronger than a human) refers to booze. *Puhaltaa yhteen hiileen* (lit. to blow on the same coal) indicates cooperation. *Napapiirin tutkija* can be translated as "polar explorer" or "navel examiner."

A "Good Morning America" program noted the word for ballpoint pen: *kuulakärkikynä*. I had not previously noted that the English "ballpoint pen" becomes "bullet-point pen" in Finnish!

Finns evidently thought the e-mail symbol "@" resembled a tabby curled up, so they called it *miukunmaukun* and *kissanhäntä* (lit. meow-meow and cat's tail) until 1998, when Finland's Standardization League adopted *ät* as the correct word. In popular lingo, it is called *ättä!*

I wondered whether there was a *Who's Who in Finland.* I found that there was, but it wasn't titled *Kuka on kuka.* It is *Kuka kukin on.* I do think the slant is what might be expected from modest Finns: afraid of sounding like "Who Really IS Somebody," Finns opted to go with something like "Who Each One Is." Finns popularly refer to the work as *Ken on ken!* In any case, no one should insist on a literal translation, because "who's who" is literal nonsense.

I am intrigued by a note in *Highlights,* the monthly newsletter of Zion Lutheran Church (formerly Suomi Zion Lutheran Church) in Fairport Harbor, Ohio. "Pastor's Finnish Bible Study" is translated not as *"Pastorin Suomenkielinen Raamattu Kerho"* but as *"Miesten Sauna Ryhmä"* ("Men's Sauna Group"). Is "Bible" in English the equivalent of "sauna" in Finnish? Is the Bible study held in a sauna? Are we dealing here with a male chauvinist organization, which doesn't allow women to join? If women were allowed to join, would it still be a Bible study? Seriously, we hope it continues to "meet on the second Thursday of each month at 7:00 p.m."

It is often difficult to convey sense from Finnish to English and vice versa. In November 2000, I tried to explain to friends in Finland about the American election with its "chads," which are bits of paper pushed through a voting card—sometimes just dimpled, sometimes left hanging, sometimes dropped. For "pregnant chads," I tried *raskaat säätit* (heavy-with-child chads) and *lasta odottavat säätit* (waiting-for-a-child chads). For dimpled chads, I tried *hymykuoppaiset säätit* (smiling pothole chads). I gave up!

By the way, did you know that St. Chad's Day is observed on March 2? Chad became Bishop of York in 665, but the archbishop invalidated Chad's consecration when Wilfrid, the more legitimate claimant, returned to England. Chad did not contest the matter but meekly submitted to the demotion. His humility so impressed the archbishop that Chad was legitimately consecrated Bishop of Mercia. The prayer for the festival of St. Chad is pertinent: "Keep us, we pray Thee, from thinking of ourselves more highly than we ought to think, and ready at all times to step aside for others, that the cause of Christ may be advanced." Calling ambiguous election scraps "chads" is logical!

Some translations may be skewed by the cultural setting. In Finnish, time "passes" *(aika kuluu);* in Spanish, time "walks" *(el tiempo anda);* in English, our clocks and watches "run"! In Latin, we are urged to "seize the day" *(carpe diem);* Hispanics are likely to say, "There is more time than life!" *(Hay mas tiempo que vida!)*

FATA becomes a suitable acronym for Finnish American Translators Association. In this day of low fat, we don't care to have it pronounced "Fat-ah" nor "Fay-tah," which sounds kind of cheesy; we prefer to have it pronounced "Fah-tah." Some of us who are into translating religious materials thought of founding a Finnish American Religious Translators organization, but the acronym didn't appeal!

Proverbs

Proverbs often indicate the personalities of the speakers. Finns are reported to have the greatest number of written proverbs of any nation. Of course, all nationalities have interesting proverbs—I like the Malay saying, "You may as well try to chop water!" Furthermore, many proverbs are claimed by a dozen nationalities. It's not a question of ownership. Different people come to the same sayings, just as different persons invent similar inventions. A proverb is a Finnish proverb if Finns resonate to it. It doesn't matter if a lot of other nationalities resonate to it also. One nation is free to adapt or to recycle or to clone those statements that come naturally from its character. There are some sayings which I think are proverbs, but I don't know if I made them up or if I heard them—for example, "He's just a pint trying to be a quart."

Many Finnish sayings have an intriguing twist of phrase:

Päivä on jo harakan askelta pitempi! (The day is already a crow's step longer!)

Minä olen viikkovillissä! (My week's gone wild on me! What day is it?)

On ollut sydän syrjällä koko viikon! (My heart's been on edge all week!)

Kävi kuin kissa kuumassa uunissa. (Stopped in like a cat in a hot oven.)

Ne ovat eri vesillä pesty! (They're washed with different waters—refers to persons who are distinctly different.)

A number of Finnish proverbs are self-deprecating:

Jos tulisi kesä ja sääskiä, että köyhilläkin olisi ystäviä! (Ah, to have summer and mosquitoes so even the poor would have friends!)

Kun vähän aikaa syö, niin katoaa koko ruokalysti! (After eating awhile, one loses his appetite!)

Omin voimin mää sinne menin, mut alas mää tulin Luojan kyytillä. (I got up there by myself, but the Lord gave me a ride down—spoken by one who falls from a tree.)

Some Finnish proverbs illustrate a no-nonsense practicality:
Auta miestä mäessä, eikä mäen päällä! (Help a person up the hill, not at the top!)

Kun syö väliin, niin ei tuu nälkäkään niin pian. (If you eat once in a while, you won't get hungry as soon.)

Kun kahta jänistä ajaa, niin ei saa yhtäkään! (If you chase two rabbits, you won't catch either one!)

Se ei ole räätäli joka ei ratko! (He's no tailor if he doesn't rip!)

Kyllä kissa kynnet löytää, kun täytyy puuhun nousta! (Of course, a cat will find claws when it needs to climb a tree!)

Istutaan vähän aikaa ja annetaan kiireen mennä ohi! (Let's sit down and let the hurry go past!)

Syöminen on ihmisen pääelinkeino. (Eating is the best way to make a living.)

Some are downright sarcastic:
Kuule, sinä senkin pölkkypää, haista napas ja paranna tapas! (Listen, you jackass, check what your belly button smells like, and shape up!)

Pitäsi pestä päätään siltä puolen missä silmät on! (One should wash his head on the side that has the eyes!)

Hän sanoo, mitä sylki suuhun tuo! (He says whatever comes into his mouth along with the spit!)

Jos sulla ei ole muuta tekemistä, niin notkuttele edes polviasi! (If you don't have anything else to do, at least flex your knees!)

Kaikkea sitä sairaan mieli tekee! (Of all the things you crave when you're sick!)

Hän on niinkuin puusta pudonnut ja vähän välillä säikähtänyt! (He's as though he'd fallen out of a tree and got scared on the way!) In America, we call that the "Duh" response!

Niinkuin toisen asialla. (As though on someone else's

business—refers to someone who doesn't seem to know what he's doing.)

Some don't make much sense:

Muun maan mustikka, oman maan mansikka. (A blueberry in one's own land, a strawberry in a foreign land.) That doesn't make sense if you like blueberries better than strawberries!

Hyvä ääni, mutta häjy villa, sano piru kun sikaa keritsi. ("It has a good voice but terrible wool," said the devil as he sheared a hog.)

Finglish

Some people are surprised to learn that English is my third language. My first language was Finnish; my second language was Finglish! Some non-Finns referred to Finglish as "Anguished English!" In *The River Midnight* by Lilian Natel, a Jewish intellectual renounces Yiddish as "the dialect of garlic." I suppose Finglish could be the dialect of cardamom coffee bread!

Finglish is to Finnish as Yiddish is to Hebrew. Just as Yiddish (derived from the German Judisch) was a fusion of Hebrew with German and other European languages, so Finglish is a fusion of Finnish and English. "Finglish" in Finnish is *fingliska* or *fingelska!*

As words segue from one language to another, they inevitably undergo changes. We English speakers anglicize the pronunciation of all languages: *Flors Heim* becomes "Florsheim," *Steinweg* becomes "Steinway!" We choose our pronunciation, for example, Des Plaines versus Des Moines. In the Finnish-American community, "Otto Mäki" became "automatic!" "Mrs." became "mörs" as Mrs. Sutinen read the Ladies' Aid minutes. Now the "Meijer" store becomes a *meijeri* (dairy)!

Finglish has even gotten into some place names. For example, Mass City, Michigan, has become "Mässetti;" New Castle, Pennsylvania, has segued to "Nakkeli;" and if you're in New York, you're "Nykissä!" As St. Louis is a city on the Mississippi River, which wends its way to the Gulf of Mexico, so Wainola is a village on Newholm Creek, which rushes on to Lake Superior. Of course, no natives called it Newholm Creek—it was, more honestly, "Mud Creek," or "Motkrikki" in Finglish.

The language Finnish immigrants came with in the late nineteenth and early twentieth centuries didn't have words for such inventions as radio, television, telephone. It was natural to pick up the English words for those items. As they began to use English on the job, downtown, and in the neighborhood, they began to fuse the English and Finnish words.

Finns learned English because that's the language on the money. No school taught English as a second language to Finn kids. The term Finglish came before Ebonics. Maybe we just weren't smart enough to start a movement for recognition of our mistakes as a new language. Bastardization of language is constant, of course. "Pidgin English" was "Business English" originally. There are "Spanglish" and lots of other "ishes" out there. Sometimes Finns speak Latin, too, as *fiikus (ficus)* for "fig tree," *pelargoni (pelargonium)* for "geranium."

Of course, Finland's Finns are now joining in Finglishizing with a vengeance. According to an article by Pertti Räty in *Amerikan Uutiset* (Aug. 12, 1998): *"Surffaiallessani netillä, serveri linkki koruptoi, printteri jammasi!"* ("Surfing on the net, the server link was corrupted, and the printer jammed!")

Many countries have banned the use of Western terms. In Iceland and Israel, foreign words are legal, but linguistic purists are constantly creating new words instead of accepting foreign terms. The following are banned in Turkey, with the threat of a fine for their use in ads or on the airwaves: cool, hot, hit. Iran bans: computer, fax, intellectual, police, secular. France has a list of 3,500 words, including: air bag, brainstorming, bulldozer, cheeseburger, log on, and stress, which can't be used in schools, agencies or companies.

"Finglish" is a Finnishing of English words, most often by

adding a vowel at the end of the word. "House" becomes *haussi,* "garage" *kraatsi,* "car" *kaara.* "Pub" becomes *Pupi,* as at Pupi Olteri, where the summer hotel Malakias served its breakfast. Somehow, an Old Testament prophet and a pub seem to have quite a generation gap. There are problems, of course. Since a Finn Hall became a *haali,* some American Finns thought the name of the Christmas plant was "holl," and that it was "holly" in Finglish! "Mall" in Finglish becomes *maali* (paint) instead of the Finnish *ostokeskus!* Sometimes, instead of adding the vowel, Finglish drops a closing consonant, as in *konstruktio, erektio,* etc.

A more complicated example of Finglish: The English word "stitch" has several problems for the Finnish pronouncer. First, it is unnatural for a word to begin with more than one consonant, so we must drop the "s" and begin with "t." The English sound "tch" is grossly un-Finnish and had best be transliterated as a simple "k." Surprise: the "i" is OK, so now we have "tik." However, nouns aren't supposed to end in consonants, so we'd better add an "i" at the end. "Stitch" has such a punch, however, that "tiki" doesn't quite do it. We'll therefore double the "k" and produce "tikki," which is regularly used in Finglish, as in *"Siihen sormeen kai pitäs panna tikki!"* ("That finger probably ought to have a stitch!")

Finglish is being exported to Finland, too. *Työryhmä* (team) has become *tiimi,* "teak" of course is *tiikki,* "make-up" is *meikki.* Instead of *taitotieto,* "know-how" is in vogue, as is "roll-on" for *kieppo,* "aerosol" for *sumute,* "deodorant" for *raikaste, homogeeninen* and *heterogeeninen* for *tasakoosteinen* and *sekakoosteinen, projekti* for *hanke, animaatio* for *elotus, bookata* for *varata, traditio* for *perinne,* "speaker" for *juontaja,* and *stressi* for *rasite* or *paine.*

Ahti Karjalainen, a former prime minister of Finland, was asked whether he had seen kangaroos when he visited an American zoo. He admitted he hadn't seen those but that he had seen "dangeroos." Well, the sign did say "Dangerous."

Finglish isn't that unique. All languages borrow from others.

English didn't invent "stadium," "beer," and "Bible." When Finns on this side of the Atlantic borrow English, it's called "Finglish;" when Finns in Finland borrow English, it's called "culture words" *(kulttuurisanoja)!* Consider *inflaatio, hakkeri, kongressi, seksi, tsaari, paralympialaiset*—all in one issue of the *Amerikan Uutiset!* Of course, the English borrowed those words from other languages first!

We talk about "Finglish," but it could be "Finndish" as well, because similar combinations are made from Swedish words: *hissi, kortti, kioski, poliisi,* even *Teerijärvi,* come from the Swedish words: *hiss, kort, kiosk, polis,* and *Terjärv!* Let's just say the Swedes mangled the Finnish words.

Some of the Finnish/English hybrids are more imaginative: "feeling" becomes *fiilis,* as in *Mull' on hyvä fiilis* (I have a good feeling); "singles" become *sinkkuja,* as in *Sekä sinkkuja että pariskuntia* (Singles as well as couples). The Helsinki fast-food restaurant Hesburger advertised *dippaillaan ranskalaiset!* (lit. Let's dip French fries!). We also saw a McDonald's advertising a McKesä (lit. a McSummer): *tuplajuustoateria, vaniljatötterö* (double cheeseburger plus vanilla cone).

As a very young child, my sister Ruth-Esther must have heard "pancakes" referred to as *pannukakut* in Finnish. Once, when the family was ordering breakfast at a restaurant, the waitress asked Ruth-Esther what she wanted. Her answer was "pannygagys." That's reverse Finglish!

Bilingualism

Most Europeans are into foreign languages much more than Americans. Americans too would no doubt learn more modern languages if they encountered a different language every time they crossed a state line. At the Lutheran World Federation assembly in Helsinki, Wittenberg University conferred an honorary doctorate on its former student, who was then Finland's Archbishop Martti Simojoki. At a banquet which followed at the Kalastajatorppa Restaurant, the honored guest was toasted in six modern languages plus Latin!

Finland has two official languages—Finnish and Swedish. Upon arriving in Helsinki, for example, the tourist notices street signs in both languages. Finland's situation is quite unique—it is the only nation which requires citizens speaking the majority language (Finnish) to learn a minority language (Swedish). The various areas in Finland are designated either Finnish-speaking unilingual, Swedish-speaking unilingual, or bilingual; the status is reviewed after each census. According to Kenneth McRae, who has done extensive research on multilingual societies in Switzerland, Belgium, Finland, and Canada: "This system of flexible territoriality has operated rather smoothly in Finland since 1922." The special status of the Swedish-speaking Åland Islands has been recognized by the European Union. Measures have also been taken for increased recognition of the Sami (Lapp) language. It should also be noted that Finnish has been approved as a minority language in Sweden, and Swedish-speaking Finns have been recognized as an ethnic minority in that land.

Since there are two national languages in Finland, the third language a citizen learns (in school, for example) becomes the person's first "foreign" language. It is therefore not surprising that Finns speak more languages than most Europeans. Sixty-two percent of Finns speak English, 52 percent Swedish, and 24 percent German. Over 68 percent of the population speaks at least a second language.

Among Finnish Americans, there is wide acceptance of Swedish-speaking Finns. At FinnFest USA, welcome signs may be printed in three languages: "Welcome, *Tervetuloa, Välkommen!*" At one opening ceremony, three national anthems were sung—those of the United States, Canada, and Finland. The first stanza of the national anthem of Finland was sung in Finnish, the second in Swedish. In fact, the anthem was originally written in Swedish! The anthem is "Maammelaulu" or "Vårtland."

Because Finnish immigration to the United States has been comparatively late, bilingualism is a gift many American Finns also have received. After attending Salolampi sessions, a certain Finn kid was bragging that he was English/Finnish bilingual. His non-Finnish buddy said, "So what, I have a bird that can parrot in three languages!"

Since there is currently much debate about declaring English the sole official language of the United States, it is good to look at the question of bilingualism. A commission was appointed in Canada in 1963 to study that country's language situation. The commission undertook studies of a dozen other countries, such as Finland, which had more than one official language. After extensive research, the commission recommended principles borrowed from Finland's Language Law of 1922. These formed the basis of Canada's federal Official Languages Act of 1969. Attempts to implement such a plan in Canada have encountered many difficulties. It seems that each nation has to develop its own best policies based on its history, its ethnic mix, and its size.

In the January 1999 editor's column of the *Finnish American Reporter*, Lynn Maria Laitala wrote, "Language has always been a politically charged issue in the United States. Even today, many Americans believe that knowing more than one language will dissolve the ties of loyalty to the country."

Immigrants from England naturally found adjustment in the new land easier than did non-English speakers. Those whose language had least relation to English had the hardest time. Finnish is not related to English or to the Germanic, Romance, or Scandinavian languages. The Swedish kid could find some relation to "one, two, three, four" from *en, tva, tre, fura,* but what could the Finnish kid do with *"yksi, kaksi, kolme, neljä?"* Some children found kind and understanding teachers, but others were humiliated, some even punished for speaking Finnish in the schoolroom. Some misguided parents felt their children would be most easily accepted as Americans if they did not teach Finnish to the youngsters. The recent push for teaching many subjects in Spanish to Spanish-speakers is not the answer; all immigrants to the United States are best served by having to learn English as soon and as fully as possible. Additional languages should be honored and taught, however, even though half of the world's population is speaking English.

Since very few other nationalities bother to learn unique Finnish, Finns have become fluent in many modern languages. However, Finns also lead the world in cultivating a dead language: Latin. Once upon a time, Latin was the universal language of educated people in the Western world. After the Reformation, the printing press, and numerous political upheavals, Latin has declined. I still studied it in high school, but few do today since science and medicine currently give it little attention. Even the Roman Catholic Church is relinquishing Latin for local vernaculars. For a while, many thought an artificial language, Esperanto, would be a world-unifying medium, but it has not caught on. English, with all its complicated conjugations and pronunciations, has become the universal language of diplomacy. However, Finland is a last bastion of Latin. The Associated Press ran an article about a Latin conference held in Jyväskylä, Finland; 220 Latin speakers from twenty-one countries showed up for the conference. The Finnish Broadcasting Company sends its program, "News in Latin" worldwide— *"Nuntii Latini Radiophoniae Finnicae Generalis."* The program covers world news, culture, science, and sports, even jazz and Elvis.

In an earlier chapter, we considered the fatherland of the Finnish people; in this chapter, we have given attention to the mother tongue and its relatives. Enough now of this Finnish language stuff—*Auf Wiedersehn! Shalom! Ciao! Amen!*

AT THE CAFÉ ENGEL, HELSINKI

Sitting alone at a table for three
    scarcely a foot and a half square
    (although much bigger in centimeters),
I look up from my "large coffee"
    and my lingonberry tart, over
    the fresh red rose in the bud vase,
out of the window of Café Engel
    (yes, "Engel," not "Engels").
On the sign jutting out from the wall
    I see an angel and one of her wings.

My eyes flow north across Senate Square
    ("Senate Building" on the east dating
    from czarist days, long before today's
    Parliament House on Mannerheim Road),
reach beyond the statue of Alexander II
    (labeled by Finns the "good czar"
    of a Russia which often oppressed),
climb up hundreds of worn granite stairs
    (granite is plentiful here,
    close to the surface everywhere),
to the gilt crosses and sun-washed statues
    of Helsinki's neo-classical "Great Church."

Locals cut across the cobbled square
    on their way to lunch or back to work.
A bus unloads a Japanese tour group
    to pose for photographs with Alexander.
One derelict shuffles aimlessly past.
    (One has to work hard at it,
    to be homeless in Finland.)

At 13 o'clock, a band of 20 players I can't hear
    escorts the changing of the guard
    (päävartionvahdinvaihto,
    if you want to say it in Finnish).

At the next table, a lady takes a cell phone
    from her purse to speak softly
    to a friend while waiting for her drink.
I place a cube of hard sugar in my mouth,
    sip the strong coffee through it
    and begin to write a letter to Esther.

Notes of a
Tourist to Finland

It may seem logical to go *down* to find roots, but Finnish Americans go *over* the Atlantic *back* to the "old country" to find their roots—the settings and records of their forebears. Finnish Americans continue to feel drawn to the land of their fathers and mothers, echoing the sentiments of novelist Pat Conroy, who once remarked about his home: "My wound is geography. It is also my anchorage, my port of call."

A Recent Trip

Realizing that time is a nonrenewable resource, my wife Esther and I decided in the summer of 1997 that it was time to visit Finland again. We know that what is farther in distance appears smaller; we are also aware that what is farther back in time, becomes less clear. I had had the opportunity to visit Finland a number of times, beginning in 1930, sometimes for extended periods, as for sabbatical leave study from the university; but it had been ten years since my wife and I had visited Finland—it was time for a refresher.

It was a good time to go, since Finland was observing the eightieth anniversary of her independence, and there was a lot going on. (By the way, did you know that 1997 also marked the ten-thousandth anniversary of marking anniversaries?) When the U.S. was eighty-seven years old, Abraham Lincoln orated about the origins of our country. When we were in Finland, I expected any minute that someone would get up and declare: "Four score years ago, our fathers brought forth in this land a new nation, conceived in liberty and dedicated to the proposition that all men are created equal." It's interesting to me to realize that at the time of Lincoln's address, the United States as a nation was about as old as Finland was at the time of our visit.

We made the trip together with son Marty, his wife, Nancy, and their son, Nate. Having flown from the U.S. to Stockholm, Sweden, we took the popular Silja Line cruise ship *Europa* from Stockholm to Turku along the beautiful archipelago on a gorgeous day. As we arrived at the Turku harbor, our daughter Esther Nelson and granddaughter Maija were there to meet us! Having a multi-generational view gave us a broad perspective from which to view matters. For the two weeks we traveled Finland, we had Spain-like weather with Windows 95 skies. Even though farmers thought it too hot and dry, it was wonderful for us tourists—we had Finntastic, suntastic days.

Since we had only two weeks, we rented a car for the quickest transportation. The driving started out on a rather sad note because when we hit the highway, the first thing we saw was a funeral procession—a dark limo followed by a long line of cars, all with their lights on. After we passed the cortege rather quietly, another funeral procession appeared with all headlights on. Since that one included a couple of logging trucks, we remembered: Ah, all motorized vehicles in Scandinavia have to have their lights on—one can't turn them off. We looked, and yes, our lights were on, too, and we sure were no funeral! I suggested that Finns could turn their car lights off for the entire summer and save batteries; they said they'd rather leave the headlights on and save lives!

At least all the traffic drove on the right side of the road, not as in England and Wales, which Esther and I had visited the previous year. We never could get accustomed to that "wrong-sided" driving. Regarding this issue, I think Sweden's experience some years back is the most amazing: After years of driving on the left, like the British, the Swedes decided to drive on the right like other Scandinavians. Can you imagine that? On such and such a date, start driving on the other side of the road! No matter that the steering wheel is in the same place! Think of driving along and wondering, "Is it now time to switch to the other side before that bus reaches me, or is my watch ahead?" To make it a little simpler, they said: "OK, we'll begin at midnight Monday, and no one drives on Sunday, except for operating emergency vehicles." Of course, there was one wag in Parliament who said: "There we go again, from one extreme to the other. Let's be moderate: the first year only trucks switch to the right!"

In Finland, we drove right. We were quickly spotted as tourists because we didn't have cell phones! For overnight accommodations, we did live it up a couple of times, but mostly we resided at "tourist hotels" (university dormitories converted to tourist use). It would not be economical to build hotels to accommodate the summer influx and then to have them stand empty during the rest of the year.

Let us review what Finland is like. A resident of Finland or a recent Finnish immigrant to the United States could give a more accurate picture of Finland, but it may be informative to have impressions of Finland as seen by a third-generation Finnish American.

Finland remains distant but easily accessible.
First of all, Finland is far north—a land north of Eden, a hinterland far "hinter" than Netherland. The northernmost country in the world after Iceland, it is as far north as Alaska. However, a Roper poll in 2001 showed that Finland is becoming better known among Americans: 86 percent actually remembered having heard of Finland, 67 percent admitted they were only slightly familiar with that country, and only 17 percent were quite familiar with her. However, what respondents knew about Finland was mainly cold, snow, ice, and darkness!

In spite of its location, Finland is easily accessible by land, air, and sea. Finns travel abroad a lot, and more tourists are finding Finland, which has been a well-kept secret until recently. In the past, unique Finland has often been bypassed even by "Scandinavia tours." Now tourists are discovering that far-northern Finland has sunlit summers and dark winters.

("Daylight savings time" in Finland's summer is a misnomer: there's enough daylight to waste all night!) In addition to Helsinki and Lapland, the Lakeland area (Järvi-Suomi) and Eastern Finland are being touted as tourist destinations.

Even in the cold winters, tourist numbers are growing, with some special attractions: a hotel made of ice, reindeer-sleighing in Lapland, and, of course, Santa's headquarters above the Arctic Circle! There is a saying in Finland, "Only two species go hatless in the streets in winter—statues and foreigners; the latter are the ones that move."

Finland Finns currently make special efforts to keep in touch with the Finnish diaspora—Finns dispersed around the world. Some years ago, the Suomi Seura, dedicated to maintaining ties between Finland Finns and other Finns, sponsored the Finnish Expatriate Parliament *(Ulkosuomalais parlamentti)* in Helsinki. Perhaps a better English term would be "Parliament for the Finnish Diaspora." Finns from twenty-seven countries, representing 131 organizations, attended the organizing convention, including thirty-four from the United States and fourteen from Canada.

Finland is a Western European democracy.
The second aspect of Finland's unique geographic location is that it has stood between Russia and Sweden, between East and West, between dictatorship and democracy. Neighbored by autocratic Russia and the kingdoms of Sweden, Norway, and Denmark, Finland surprisingly has a western political style—an elected president and parliament. Its location has sparked an interesting history, produced a unique language, and developed a resilient people.

Wislawa Szymborska, the Polish Nobel winner, writes:
"Each of us wished to have a homeland
with no neighbors
and to live one's entire life
in the intervals between wars."

Life free of bordering neighbors has been granted only to places like New Zealand. It was not granted to Finns, who have had interesting neighbors and more than their share of wars. Henry James once remarked that being an American was a "complex fate." He should have tried being a Finn!

The Finns lived as independent tribes until conquered in 1216 by the Kingdom of Sweden, which accorded Finns equal rights with Swedes. In 1809, Finland became a grand duchy of Russia, with Helsinki as its administrative and cultural center. Czar Alexander I promised to uphold the Lutheran faith and the constitutional laws of the area. Finns obviously didn't take to Russianness during more than a century of rule. Following the Russian Revolution of 1917, Finland became a sovereign state.

Finland has a far longer border with Russia than does any other bordering nation, but it looks to the West for kindred nations. A foreign correspondent once asked a Finn: "Do you consider the Russians your friends or brothers?" "Brothers, of course. We choose our friends!"

In October 1939, the Soviet Union pressured Estonia, Latvia, and Lithuania to accept Soviet garrisons. Finland, however, resisted. The Soviets invaded Finland on November 30, 1939. Subsequently, the Soviet Union complained about Finland's part in the war of 1939–40, saying, in effect: "He hit me back first!"

During the Second World War, Finland and the Soviet Union resumed hostilities in 1941–44. Finland at first regained its lost territory quickly and gained control of considerable new territory in Eastern Karelia. In response, the Soviet Union attacked on the Karelian Isthmus with overwhelming forces. Finnish forces had to retreat, and Finland had to sign a peace treaty which gave the Soviet Union the islands of the eastern Gulf of Finland, the Salla area, most of Karelia, and the Petsanga area. Furthermore, Finland was forced to lease out the Porkkala Peninsula near Helsinki and pay huge war reparations.

A Finnish veteran explained to me how the fight against the Russian forces became just impossible: "Professor, it was like farting at a skunk. What chance have you got?"

Finland was also compelled to drive the German troops out of northern Finland. Finland did manage to retain her independence and democratic government. No other country, which had gained independence after World War I, succeeded in maintaining its independence. However, the nation had tremendous challenges for a decade: war reparations, reconstruction, food shortages, and relocation of evacuees.

Finland's eastern border these days is peaceful but guarded. Russian President Yeltsin once proposed joint surveillance of the border in the interests of cost savings. In light of countless border problems throughout Finland's history, then President Ahtisaari said, "Thanks, but no thanks—let each country take care of its own security!"

Back in 1987, when my wife and I visited the Finnish/Russian border at Imatra, Esther had hoped to take a photo of the guard station but saw a sign forbidding picture taking. When she mentioned her disappointment to the guard, he said, "Come with me right over here, and your husband can take a picture of us under that sign!"

We also had an interesting adventure at the Finnish/Russian border in 1997. The highway goes very close to the border at Parikkala and Kolmekanta, so we drove there, got out of the car and stood looking over the no-man's land between two countries. A uniformed soldier from a nearby observation tower drove up on a motorcycle and spoke pleasantly with us, explaining clearly that we should not go beyond certain markers because such trespassing would set off alarms on both sides of the border. We have a photo of the border guard with his arm around our grandson Nate, both standing at the border defended years ago by previous generations of Finns.

We've come a long way from days when Finland and the United States were technically enemies. During World War II, Finland was at war with our ally, the Soviet Union. I remember when Finland's Ambassador Hjalmar Procopé was asked to leave the United States. He asked me to see him embark from New York Harbor and to pray for him, for Finland, and for our land. His comment was touching: *"Onhan aina ilo palata koti-maahan. Mutta tässä tilanteessa se on niin vaikeaa!"* ("Of course, it's always good to return to one's homeland, but in this instance, it's so painful!")

Finns try to live at peace with their neighbors, but they have not had the luxury of pacifism. The experiences of war and its ravages are still seared into the nation's consciousness. I have relatives and friends in Finland who bear the real scars of war in their bodies and minds. Currently, however, there is a period of relaxed tensions between Finland and her neighbors.

We have noted that, before becoming a grand duchy within Russia, Finland was part of Sweden for centuries. Relations with Sweden these days are very good, but there is a natural rivalry also. The story is told of a regional athletic meet held in Helsinki. The primarily Finnish audience had its favorites, of course, but in one race, in which a Russian and a Swede were pitted against each other, virtually no one cheered for either contestant!

A good illustration of peaceful coexistence is the Green Zone Golf Club in Tornio. Its course could be called the Seven-Eleven because the main course has seven holes in Finland, eleven in Sweden. It isn't necessary to show a passport each time a national border is crossed, but one can have it stamped. Several greens are divided by a time zone as well as by the national border, making it possible to sink a one-hour putt or to make a hole-in-one in an hour and four seconds! (By the way, do you know why golf courses have eighteen holes? The Scots, who invented the game, claimed there are eighteen sips in the flask, so it makes sense to have eighteen holes at which to stop. They didn't need a nineteenth hole lounge!)

The Finnish flag has a Scandinavian pattern—a cross displayed against a field. The Finnish flag's blue-on-white colors, however, had been symbols of the Finnish people for decades before independence. Already in the 1860s, when Finland was a grand duchy of Russia, the sky-blue cross on a snow-white field was displayed in a variety of contexts.

Geographically and historically, the "chosen" Israelites were led to a critical spot between Asia and Africa and Europe and Africa. Finns have been set at the juncture of East and West, and also chosen to play a historic role. Of course, there are many nations which are at geographic pressure points, destined by location to be at important junctures in international relations. For all those nations, the basic question is: how have their roles been played?

Finland remains internationally involved.
Geography makes Finland seem far from everyone, yet she has been and still is an active participant in world affairs. Early in 2001, *Foreign Policy Magazine* published results of a study by A.T. Kearney, showing that Finland was the world's fifth most "global" country, as evidenced by her integration with neighbors through the cross-border flow of goods and services, capital, people, and communication. The Globalization Index collects data from fifty developed countries and key emerging markets, representing more than 95 percent of the world's economic output.

A factor which facilitates international connections is airport service. For years, the Helsinki/Vantaa airport has been listed as one of the world's premier airports in customer satisfaction.

Finland joined the United Nations and the Nordic Council in 1955. In 1961, she became an associate member of the European Free Trade Association, EFTA. The Agreement on Security and Cooperation in Europe was signed in Helsinki in 1975. The follow-up conference for the agreement was held in Helsinki also, in 1991.

Finland is a member of the European Union; in fact, Finland

was the first country to join the union. Did that "first" happen because she was spearheading the movement? Because she was the most pushy? No, it happened because Finland was in the easternmost time zone of the countries involved!

Finnish and American troops regularly cooperate in peace-keeping operations. Finland regularly provides peacekeepers to the United Nations for the trouble spots of our world.

A former president of Finland, Martti Ahtisaari, received the J. William Fulbright Prize for International Understanding in 2000 and also was nominated for the Nobel Peace Prize. Frederick G. Acker, president of the Fulbright Association's Board of Directors, said, "President Ahtisaari is one of the great peacemakers of the twentieth century. He has spent much of his distinguished career brokering solutions to seemingly hopeless conflicts in Namibia, Kosovo, and Northern Ireland. Namibia so appreciated his efforts over thirteen years in achieving their peaceful independence that they granted him honorary citizenship."

Finland continues to be a bridge between East and West for the world in the new millennium, hosting meetings between these regions.

Ted Turner may have been born Teuvo Törmä. As you know, he saved the United Nations' finances singlehandedly a few years ago. As Paavo Harvi would say, "Let me tell you the rest of the story." Turner met Kofi Annan, secretary-general of the United Nations, who evidently speaks Finnish too. Ted said, *"Annan!"* (which can also mean "I'll give!") Kahvi asked, *"Kuinka paljon?"* ("How much?") Ted was on the spot, and didn't want to appear cheap, so he said, *"Biljoonan!"* ("A billion!")

Finland is a fascinating combination of the old and the new.
Finland has an ancient culture, as evidenced by its many historic landmarks. Evidence of human habitation in Finland goes back

over 9,000 years. The oldest settlement in Finland, Ristola in Lahti, recently has been dated to 8000 B.C. on the basis of a flint knife and other evidence of toolmaking. Since thousands of items have been found, the settlement is considered to have included hundreds of people.

Many of Finland's cities juxtapose ancient buildings with the most modern of architecture. In the United States, ruins are to be destroyed, but in Finland, as in much of Europe, ruins are considered beautiful, nostalgic—reminding us of history. Thus, one finds cities with civility in Finland.

Finland has been on the map of Europe for 500 years. However, as a nation, Finland is young compared to Britain or Egypt, for example. It has been independent only since 1917. Finnish Americans speak often about the "old country," as though the United States were the young one. However, the United States is over two hundred years old, whereas Finland is not yet ninety! Of course, Finland is a generation older than Israel, which is in her fifties! Finland is only two years older than I am, and it is younger than Jesse Helms! So let's try to think of middle-aged America and youthful Finland.

On the one hand, Finland's cities have good public transportation; on the other, there still are cobblestone streets. Walking on cobblestones isn't easy, especially for those with high heels, but cobblestones are giving way to paving in many areas.

On a highway, a tourist may see Finns roller-skiing along the berm, but may also see evidence of high technology. (Incidentally, are roller-skiers vehicular or pedestrian traffic?) Video cameras monitor speed on certain highways—the cameras photograph speeding cars, and authorities send tickets to offending drivers. Fines can be paid at banks by money card! Even some moose crossings are monitored by radar: when moose are crossing a highway at their accustomed crossing areas, moose signs begin to flash 300 meters before the area, warning drivers that moose are present. The cost of each such warning device is about $50,000. One of the devices between Helsinki and Porvoo had to be re-engineered because the first installation was being triggered by horses grazing near the highway!

In literature, Finns are fond of the ancient *Kalevala* and the current Moomins. They are avid readers of standard newspapers and books, but they also use advanced information technology.

In music, Finland has seen a recent Sibelius revival but also a Linda (Lampenius) Brava craze.

Finns still drink *sima* (mead) and *kalja* (near beer), but Hartwall Company, the leading soft drink purveyor, has been a long-time partner with Coca-Cola.

Surprisingly, faraway Finland has been a trendsetter in many areas. It was ahead of the United States in Prohibition—and its repeal. Even the Depression started early in Finland, in 1928!

Finland is an interesting mix of city and countryside.
Although it is the sixth-largest country in Europe, Finland is still a small country of 130,000 square miles, smaller than the state of Montana. Stretching 721 miles from north to south, 336 miles from east to west, it has a population comparable to that of Indiana or of metropolitan Chicago—slightly over five million. When my wife, Esther, taught social studies in junior high school, she dramatically spoke of gallant little Finland standing up to the huge Russian bear. She wondered whether she had overdone the drama when, in correcting test papers, she found the answers were regularly "little Finland," instead of "Finland!"

A Texas oil tycoon became so intrigued with "little Finland" that he flew there to get to know it better. When his host, Onni, spoke about cross-country skiing, the Texan commented, "I suppose cross-country's OK if you've got a country small enough to ski across!"

The story doesn't end there. The Texan wanted to return the favor and invited Onni to Texas *(vastavierailulle)*. At the Texan's ranch, the Finn was impressed by the huge room, the big people, the mammoth martinis, the lavish table, and the huge steak. He inquired where the bathroom was and was told to go out of the dining room, down the hall to the left, and to take the second door on the right. Onni went down the block-long hall and, in spite of the martinis, tried to follow directions. Well, he must have taken a wrong turn somewhere, because as he careened through the door, he fell into a white-tiled swimming pool. Onni panicked and yelled, "Don't flush!"

Finland is the land of Finns and of low-lying fens or swamps. The name can be interpreted as "Finn-land" or as "fen-land." The Finnish word *"Suomi"* could also have been written *"Suomaa,"* meaning "marsh-land." Think of marshes and snow—Finland is often a marshmallow-land!

Besides marshlands, however, there are rock outcroppings, as in Helsinki, the nation's capital. I understand the Irish have sham-rocks. Finns have real rocks—granite!

Finland's forests are well managed. Even though it produces one-fourth of the world's paper and wood products, Finland does it by using less than 1 percent of its forested land. There is a sur-prisingly high level of cooperation between those concerned with timber production on the one hand and those who defend recre-ation and wildlife on the other.

Like many industrialized nations, Finland is becoming more urbanized. Eighty percent of its population lives in towns and cities. However, the cities are relatively small: Helsinki has half a million and the next four cities less than three hundred thousand each. Between towns and cities are large evergreen forests, the pine tuning forks resonating to the wind. Moreover, the cities and towns are full of parks and greenways. Birches, mountain ash, and junipers flourish in the yards. Interestingly, granite may crop out in a park or in the middle of a housing development.

Finland has more private holiday residences per capita than any other nation—430,000 summer homes for a population of slightly more than five million. Those summer residences are usually near lakes. Summer homes make sense in a society where practically all wage and salary earners receive at least two days of paid vacation for every month worked. During the second year of work, the standard is two and a half days per month worked. Thus, five-week vacations are common, with six-week vacations available for those employed for fifteen years.

Perhaps all nationalities would love nature as much as Finns do if they had as beautiful a country. It's a high-sky country of lowlands. Finland has nearly two hundred thousand lakes. Esther thinks it's a body of water that has lots of islands. Generally, we say that Finland has lots of lakes, and those lakes have countless islands. Throughout the land, there are huge forests of evergreens, which are managed for continued harvest but not depletion. The birches there grow as large as oaks. Furthermore, the forests, lakes, and waterways are clean. Tampere is Finland's Manchester (England), without belching factory smoke!

There is a town named Interlochen (between lakes) in Michigan, and Switzerland has its Interlaken between Lake Thun and Lake Brienz. Traveling in Finland, one has the feeling that half of its towns could be named *Järvenväli* (between lakes). The large lakes of southern Finland—Saimaa, Päijänne, Keitele, and Näsijärvi—are great for boating or sightseeing by passenger ship.

Finland is traditional but egalitarian.
Finnish society is economically very egalitarian, with the smallest gap between richest and poorest of any Western nation. According to a 2000 study by the United Nations Children's Fund, Finland is one of only five nations which has less than 5 percent of its children living in relative poverty (households with incomes below 50 percent of the national median).

Governmental and church leaders have publicly opposed corporate management stock option schemes. Instead of faulting their government for taking tax money that belongs to them, Finnish citizens tend to speak of their nation serving them by providing for the needs of all. To meet the needs of society's most needy, Finland regularly has one of the highest tax rates of industrial countries.

Consider Jaakko Rytsola, who was caught speeding—19 mph over the speed limit! He had to pay the fine, and it was $70,600. Why so high? Fines in Finland are based on the rate of speed and the financial status of the offender. Since Rytsola is a millionaire, the system really socked it to him. He paid his debt, taking it all in good humor: "The road was wide, and I was feeling good!"

An example of Finland's concern for welfare is Helsinki's soup program for children begun in 1951. Since almost every child lives within one kilometer of a playground, free soup is provided to thirteen thousand children five days a week, June through August, at sixty-two playgrounds across the city. Helsinki also allows a parent with a child in a carriage or stroller free rides on public transport. Furthermore, there are numerous free sports activities for children at five hundred sport venues.

In England, there was much discussion of whether Tony Blair should take parental leave after the birth of his fourth child in May 2000. Tony's wife, Cherie, noted that Finnish Prime

Minister Paavo Lipponen had set a fine example by taking six days of parental leave after his wife Paivi gave birth to their second daughter. Lipponen hadn't agonized about his decision, because he had already taken parental leave for the birth of his first child! Two out of three fathers in Finland take paternal leave. Men are entitled to take up to eighteen days of fully paid paternity leave; women are entitled to 105 days of maternity leave. I don't know why the Finns still have such gender inequality in some matters!

Gender equality has been achieved more in Finland than in most other western societies. Finland was the first European country to give women the vote, in 1906. (By comparison, the United States adopted the nineteenth Amendment in 1920). Actually, Finland wasn't even a country yet—it was still a grand duchy of Russia. Some proud Finn remarked, "Finland may have been a duchy, but it was a grand one!" Although part of Russia, it was granted considerable autonomy until it became an independent nation in 1917. In 1907, in their first opportunity to hold political office, nineteen women were elected to the 200-member parliament. Currently, the Finnish Parliament has the highest percentage of women members of any nation in the world. Telephone directories consistently list the wife's name as well as the husband's, for example, "Hillila, Bernhard and Esther."

Finland was also early in opening academic doors to women although it was a part of Russia at the time. Higher education for women became available by the 1860s. From 1870, women were admitted to the University of Helsinki. Although architecture remained a closed field to women in Europe and even other Nordic countries, six Finnish women began their studies in Helsinki Polytechnic's Department of Architecture. By 1908, fourteen women had graduated with degrees in architecture from Helsinki Polytechnic, which at that time became the Helsinki University of Technology. In contrast, the first woman graduate in architecture in Sweden was in 1919, in Norway, 1921.

If we call a nation "she," its leader certainly could be a "she," even in the United States! In Finland's last presidential election, four of the seven declared candidates were women: Elisabeth Rehn, Tarja Halonen, Riitta Uosukainen, and Heidi Hautala. Tarja Halonen won and was inaugurated as the nation's eleventh president and first woman president.

Whoever is elected president in Finland severs party affiliation upon election. Upon her election, Tarja Halonen, a Social Democrat during the election campaign, followed this Finnish custom. That seems a good approach, removing the president somewhat from party labels.

Women have been prominent in Finnish design: Tuula Falk, wood furniture; Brita Flander, glass; Kristina Riska, ceramics; Janna Syvänoja, recycled paper; and Ulla-Maija Vikman, textiles, are some of the current stars.

Ethnically, Finland's population is noticeably homogeneous. Of course, there are the minority inhabitants, such as Lapps and Gypsies. Recently, the situation has begun to change with the influx of immigrants from areas such as Bosnia and Somalia. Finland is trying to eliminate prejudice against such minorities.

Finland's provinces have been re-aligned recently from twelve to five in the interest of better balance. Can you imagine states in the United States having their boundaries and sizes changed? It might make sense not to have differences as great as those between Alaska and Rhode Island, but such rearranging isn't going to happen. Nor will counties allow states to change their borders.

Finland is the world's most Lutheran country.
Finland's state church, the Evangelical Lutheran Church of Finland, is the third-largest Lutheran body in the world, with 4,600,000 members. (Sweden is the first largest with 7,500,000; the Evangelical Lutheran Church in America is second with 5,200,000.) Eighty-seven percent of Finns belong to the ELCF; a minority are affiliated with the Eastern Orthodox Church. It is

reported that only 3 to 5 percent attend church every Sunday, only 10 to 12 percent attend once a month. Those statistics are misleading, however, since there is much worship activity in more informal services held in homes or meeting halls.

Some Christian contacts were made with Finland in the eleventh and twelfth centuries, but the first organized crusade was in 1155. Bishop Henry from England stayed in Finland after the crusade but was murdered by a Finn by the name of Lalli, who didn't approve of foreign religious influences. Henry is now the patron saint of Finland.

Michael Agricola was one of the Finnish theological students who studied at Wittenberg, Germany, under Luther and Melanchthon. He became archbishop and led the Reformation in Finland in a very peaceful way. The service was changed from Latin to Finnish; prayers to Mary and other saints were eliminated; priests were allowed to marry; communicants received wine as well as bread. There were no great Roman Catholic versus Lutheran or Reformed versus Lutheran conflicts. The apostolic succession remained, and pastors continued to serve the same parishes.

Five revival movements—Pietists, Laestadians, Praying Revival members, Evangelicals, and more recent Anglo-American Evangelicals—have influenced spiritual life in Finland. Significantly, all of the movements have stayed within the ELCF, rather than breaking away as separate entities. Adherents to these revival movements often meet for informal worship meetings, which include devotional messages by pastors and laity as well as hymns and spiritual songs.

The separation of church and state is only a token. Government officials participate in public worship on official festival days. When I did research on the schools of Finland, I was asked on occasion to lead the morning worship in the public schools using the Finnish Lutheran hymnal! Religion classes in those schools prevent a religious illiteracy of the population. One or two weeks before confirmation, the church offers confirmation camps, usually held in the summer at camps or retreat centers. Surprisingly, over 90 percent of Finnish youths participate, reviewing the basics of Christian doctrine and liturgy, with frank discussions about God, the meaning of life, careers, relationships, sex, and drugs.

A nation which is contemplative by nature and loves the solitude of Nature will have many spiritually sensitive members. Resonating to the mythic *Kalevala* and responding to Scripture, Finns value their spiritual heritage. We are all judged by what we have been given, and Finns have been given much in religious heritage.

Church buildings can be centuries old or very modern. Instead of a steeple on top of the church, there is usually a separate bell tower near the church.

In Turku, I asked why the cathedral was called a *tuomiokirkko.* What judgment or *tuomio* was associated with it? I was enlightened: No, the word comes from the Latin *domus,* which means "home," as in "domestic" or "domicile." That's beautiful: the cathedral is the home church of the bishop. It is the home church of the parishioners. The information was particularly fitting because Tampere University's summer hotel, Domus, was our home for the night. Home can be a movable place. The church was our spiritual home wherever we went. And it is not a place of judgment but of acceptance by God and His people, a place of God's grace and human fellowship. From now on, the cathedral will be a "home church" to me!

How does Finnishness reveal itself in Finland's church services? First of all, the procedures are well organized: Services in all six hundred local parishes begin at 10:00 a.m. Freewheeling insertions, such as kiddie chats, are not tolerated.

Finns are reticent by nature, and, therefore, they are somewhat slow about participation in the liturgy. Prayers are always said by the pastor, the congregation simply responding with "Amen." Some Finns find it awkward to respond with "Thanks be to God" after the readings. Perhaps the Finnish translation, *kiitos Jumalalle,* gives an impression of some overly emotional charismatics or entertainment spirituality.

Finns don't speak much body language, so during the service there is little signing of the cross, little standing, and no kneeling except at the altar rail for communion. In a recent article in *Cross Accent,* Pastor Jari Jolkkonen writes: "Many Finns feel that sharing peace by shaking hands and saying some formal words to their neighbors is insincere, unnatural, and intrusive." A non-Finn claims that even when the church is full of people, Finns sit fewer to a pew than non-Finns! Finns don't make the sign of the cross even when they're at bat in baseball!

Music is a very important part of the Finnish service. At least six hymns are sung during the service. Jolkkonen writes:
> "The melodies are comparatively slow and melancholic, but the texts are full of spiritual consolation and longing for future joy. These characteristics have evolved from the harsh nature of life which has always defined the Finnish mind and way of living, especially the long, dark and cold winter. Finnish life has traditionally been a struggle with and against bitter nature, sickness, suffering, isolation, and loneliness, madness and death, and, sometimes, even hunger. There was no room for any spiritual entertainment."

At the close of a church service, instead of getting out of the pews and chatting with others while going out, Finnish worshippers listen to the postlude in silence.

Throughout Finland, "road churches" are readily available. The open-door churches near busy highways offer travelers opportunities for rest, devotions, personal counseling. Many offer devotions at noon and in the evening. Official road signs point to available road churches. Maps showing the church locations are available, as is information on the Internet.

As befits a nation on the cutting edge of technology, one can also find a "Net pastor" on the Internet!

Finland is a wordstruck nation.
There are several reasons for the Finnish love of words, but one prominent factor is the religious orientation of the population. It is no mere coincidence that Finland is the most book-loving country in the world—and the most Lutheran. Even the non-churched owe some of their love of literature to their religious heritage!

The Protestant Reformation of the early 1500s placed the authority for religious teaching in a book (the Bible) rather than in a person (the pope and other clergy). And the way to relate to a book is to read it! The church used some ingenious ways to get the people to read: *kinkerit* (annual literacy testing sessions conducted by the pastor and *lukkari* in each village and town), confirmation classes, and since the 1700s, a literacy requirement for getting married! (And that was before there were any prenuptial agreements to read!) Literature for the masses really began with the invention of the printing press in 1543, just as the Reformation was getting underway.

The report "Educational Policy Analysis 2001" by the Organization for Economic Cooperation and Development rated Finland's education system the best of the eighteen industrial countries surveyed. Like the education systems of all modern countries, Finland's schools are currently being challenged and will have to work hard to remain excellent.

All of the Nordic nations rank at the top in literacy, and Finland seems to be the champion in reading. More books are bought per capita in Finland than in any other country. Books are borrowed as well as bought—there are more than four hundred libraries in Helsinki alone! It was announced in July 2000 that the Bill and Melinda Gates Foundation had given $1 million as an "Access to Learning" award to the Helsinki City Library in recognition of its promotion of the use of the Internet. In March 2000, Finland Post released a sheet of five postage stamps dedicated to Donald Duck and reading.

Those who, in past ages, preserved oral epic poems were illiterate lovers of fine literature. Some 1,500,000 lines of oral poetry—the epic *Kalevala*, the lyric *Kanteletar*, and others—were preserved in remote areas of Finland. Thus, from the beginning of available literature, Finns were with it. The oral treasure became available in printed form only in the early 1830s.

The *Kalevala*, with no pretense of divinely inspired canonical Scripture, covers the time period of the Old Testament—from Creation to the birth of Jesus. That epic poem has inspired Jean Sibelius in music, Akseli Gallen-Kallela in art, and countless others. Unique among epic poems, the *Kalevala* does not glorify war or royalty. Finland is the only nation which has a national holiday commemorating its national epic—*Kalevala* Day, on February 28. As one might expect, the epics of other lands have been translated into Finnish. What may be more surprising is that the *Kalevala* has been translated into forty-four languages, including Latin!

Finland is also a promoter of the arts.
Having already considered literature, we shall focus now on the other arts. Finland spends more public money per capita on arts and museums than any other country, according to a 1998 report by Britain's Arts Council. Only Germany comes close. One example is the action taken in Helsinki in December 1999 to give all ninth-graders passes for free or reduced admission to twenty-five cultural institutions, including symphonies, museums, and theatres. Designated as a European City of Culture for 2000, Helsinki offered over four hundred special events.

Theatre

According to Jytte Jensen, associate film and video curator at New York's Museum of Modern Art, "Current Finnish films are replete with amazingly poetic imagery—derived from or enhanced by music as well as the beauty of exotic landscapes." Some of the current movers in Finnish film are Aki Louhimies, Markku Pölönen, and Markku Lehmuskallio.

The American television program "The Bold and the Beautiful" (*Kauniit ja rohkeat*) is quite the rage in Finland, with many visits there by the stars of the program. By the way, notice that in the Finnish title, beauty comes before boldness!

Music

The Finnish national anthem, "Maamme-laulu," written by Finnish national poet Johan Ludvig Runeberg, was set to music by Fredrik Pacius, considered the father of Finnish music. It was first performed in 1848. Therefore, although Finland is only eighty years old, its national anthem is almost twice as old! That may be one more indication of strong national identity! Originally written in Swedish as "Vårtland," it was translated into Finnish by Paavo Cajander half a century later, in the 1890s. Introduced into Estonia in 1869, the song is now also the Estonian national anthem as "Mu isamaa."

Starting with one symphony orchestra in the 1920s (the Helsinki Philharmonic), Finland now, with a population of only five million, boasts fifteen orchestras, many more comparably than any of the Scandinavian countries.

In the opera world of 2000, the *New York Times* ranked composer Kaija Saariaho and soprano Karita Mattila among the best in the world.

The cover of the November 1999 issue of *BBC Music Magazine* had a teasing line, "How the Finns swept to podium power." Editor Helen Wallace introduced the discussion of why Finland has produced so many outstanding Finnish conductors with an editorial titled "Conduct Becoming" and wrote:

> "The [conducting teacher] whose students have consistently outperformed anyone else's in the last two decades is Jorma Panula of Helsinki's Sibelius Academy. His students include Esa-Pekka Salonen, Jukka-Pekka Saraste, Sakari Oramo, Osmo Vänskä and the young prodigy Mikko Franck. A humorous, unassuming character, he has been described as the great liberator of talent, producing a band of musicians notable for their lack of show, their disarming integrity and refreshing relationship with new music. . . . But some believe that Finnish society, with its profound commitment to music, has been the real promoter of talent."

The *New Yorker* magazine carried an article, "The Finnish Crescendo," which noted that the world's classical music "is being overrun by Finns . . . a country of only five million people has produced a disproportionate number of the world's leading singers, three conductors of major symphony orchestras and various composers of international stature. The music of Jean Sibelius, the country's national musical hero, has regained most of the tremendous international popularity that it enjoyed earlier in the century." The article further pointed out that music plays a vital role in the cultural life of Finland, where composers and performers are treated as folk heroes. The government continues to allocate 14 percent of its budget to education, research, and culture, an amount much greater than in most other Western countries.

Also, Finland has the world's only Latin-singing jazz band, Reine Rimon Eiusque Papae Fervidissimi (Reine Rimon and Her Hot Pipes). Linguistically proficient Finns are much more into classical languages than we Americans are.

The tango is the most popular form of ballroom dancing in Finland. The fact that it originated in Argentina is not considered a drawback. After all, the potato originated in Peru, and consider how Finns love it too! Tango lyrics, which have become part of Finnish culture, express the same emotional qualities as folk poetry. Dr. Pirjo Kukkonen has written a book, *Tango Nostalgia: The Language of Love and Longing*. Finnish tango lyrics do speak of love, sorrow, nature, the search for happiness. The most popular tango recently has been "Satumaa" (fairy tale land), which is about a far-off land beyond the sea, where flowers always bloom. Only birds reach that land, however, while humans remain earthbound. The lyrics of paradise lost and love unrequited are set to a solemn, hymn-like tune. That tango has become so popular that one theologian suggested, tongue-in-cheek, that it be included in the Finnish Lutheran hymnal!

The kantele is the national instrument of Finland, available in 5-, 15-, 36-, and 41-string versions. I remember kantele players participating in churches I served—they played at midweek programs, services, and concerts.

Finns have kept current with musical trends throughout the years; for example, there was the Scott Joplin disciple, who composed "Dishrag," "Rag-carpet Rag," and "Dust Rag"!

Visual Art
Visual art, too, is valued by Finns. Finland has the highest number of museums per capita of any nation in the world: one for every five thousand inhabitants. While in Finland, we went to the Matisse exhibit in Retretti, that wonderful underground arts center; saw Artist Veijo Rönkkönen's "Patsas Puisto" (Sculpture Garden) at Parikkala and his carvings at Lusto, and watched glass horses being made at the Nuutajärvi glassworks. We acquired a few modest artworks: a print by Juhani Palmu, a print of Gunnar Berndtson's "Kesä," and a glass bird from Nuutajärvi.

Recently, artworks made of lights have been installed along the highways near Porvoo. Also recently, a new museum of contemporary art, Kiasma (Gr. for crosspiece), opened in downtown Helsinki as the latest manifestation of Finnish innovative architecture. Called a pumpkin or a nuclear submarine by detractors, it is being appreciated as a significant "architectonic" achievement. Besides visual art, the museum will host modern dance and experimental theatre.

Design

Finland has long been a leader in design. Anja Miller explained to me what is meant by the phrase "Scandinavian product": "It is designed by the Finns, manufactured by the Swedes, sold by the Danes, and shipped by the Norwegians." Some detractors have claimed that, in place of napkins, Finns invented long shirt sleeves, but we know and constantly read about Finnish leadership in the world of clothing style.

A recent issue of *Newsweek* gave words of high praise to Finnish design:

> "For 600 [700!] years, Finland was under the thumb of either Sweden or Russia; it didn't gain independence until 1917. Maybe that's why, of all the brands of modern Scandinavian design, Finland's is the most fiercely rooted in its own folk culture and indigenous materials. But it has cast a long shadow. Finnish design of the 1930s and '40s influenced practically everything that we Americans consider *our* best modern stuff—from Charles Eames's plywood chairs to Jack Lenor Larsen's cheerful woven fabrics."

Currently, Finland is a leader in design of electronic equipment, such as mobile phones, computers, and televisions. Fiskars scissors are well known throughout the world. Sporting goods from skiing and hockey equipment to indoor exercise equipment have gained international acceptance. Finnish design has also become respected in designs for medical equipment and work safety equipment.

Finland has unique sports interests.
Finns generally have an interest in sports, especially those that do not produce millionaires. They are into long-distance running, javelin throwing, hammer throwing, triple jumping, powerlifting rather than golf, tennis, or basketball. They even play baseball in their own way. We'll note just a few examples to illustrate Finnish sports interests.

The emphasis in Finland is on community or county teams instead of school-related sports activities. As a result, sports involvement has a greater carryover to life after school years. Times to run or ski as a group are posted, with invitations to the general public to join. These affairs are not races but fitness jaunts. A high percentage of the people are in good physical shape, with a relatively low number of grossly obese folks. The emphasis is clearly on endurance rather than finesse. Was it Leo Durocher who said, "Finnish guys last nicely!"

In 1924, Paavo Nurmi won four gold medals at the Paris Olympics. Finns continue to get medals in running. For example, on June 10, 2000, in Turin, Italy, the Finnish gold medalist was Wilson Kirwa, a native Kenyan but now a Finnish citizen!

Finns are also into strength events. In 1998, Jouko Ahola won the World's Strongest Man competition. Anna-Liisa Prinkkala, 28, was listed in 1998 by *USA Powerlifting Magazine* as the all-time top woman powerlifter in the world. Raija Koskinen and Leena Jokitalo are other top contenders in women's powerlifting. As you might expect, the mighty Finnish women do well in the hammer throw, with Mia Strömmer, Sini Pöyry, and Kaisa Kiintonen leading the pack.

Mikael Saleva was the overpowering winner in wheelchair javelin at the Handicapped World Track and Field Championships in 1998. He holds the world record at 29.88 meters.

Finland's winters lead to winter sports more naturally than do the winters of Samoa. Skiing and ski jumping are big, of course. In 1999, cross-country skier Mika Myllylä was voted Finland's Sports Personality of the Year. Matti Hautamäki has been a leader in World Cup skiing. (Downhill skiing you would expect, but did you know that there's uphill skiing, too—skiers in Lapland blown uphill with parachutes!)

Hockey is popular also, producing many world-class players. During the 2000-2001 season, thirty-six Finns (thirty-four from Finland, one from Sweden, one from Canada) were on the rosters of the National Hockey League of the United States and Canada.

There are more exotic sports events also. In April 2000, Finland hosted the European Snowball Fight Championship. It is also estimated that five hundred thousand Finns have tried ice swimming, with eighty-thousand participating regularly. Some claim the practice combats colds and stress. I guess I'd just as soon have a little stress!

On February 26, 2000, Finland held the first annual Ice Pool Swimming World Championships, attracting twelve hundred competitors from eighteen nations, which included Turkey, Kazakhstan, and Japan. Various age groups competed in 25-yard and 50-yard breaststroke races held in a huge six-lane ice hole cut into the frozen sea near Helsinki's rowing stadium, which was built for the 1952 Olympics. At race time, the water temperature was 30 degrees F, but the air temperature was at a windy 19 degrees! Contestants began the races by standing on underwater platforms, which left only heads and shoulders above water. Participants were allowed to wear caps but not to use any "external or internal substances" to keep warm. After the race, however, brandy toasts were available, as were six saunas made of ice!

Surprisingly, Finns are in the front of the pack in auto racing. On January 15, 1999, the Finnish postal service issued a three-mark postage stamp featuring the world champion Formula-1 race driver, Mika Häkkinen. Another Finnish racing star, Tommi Mäkinen, won his fourth straight World Rally Driving Championship in Australia in 1999; at that point, of twenty-one contests, Finns had won eleven!

In Finland, there also are wife-carrying competitions. I think the Finnish is more expressive: *Akankantokilpailu!* (A recent newspaper article complained that the contest should be called *Eukonkantokilpailu,* but I think the other wording more poetic.) I teased a lady: "If there's such gender equality in Finland, why not have husband-carrying?" "Oh, we've always had to carry the men, beginning with carrying them in the womb!"

A recent addition to competition among Finns is boot-throwing. The competition got started when a young couple from the boonies took a shortcut to the parsonage to make their wedding vows. The problem was that they had to wade through a swampy area infested by snakes. The gallant groom offered to walk to the other side and throw his boots back for the bride to pull on and follow him. That gallantry so fired the imagination of the townsfolk that everyone began to practice boot-throwing. I thought you'd get a boot out of hearing how boot-throwing got started.

Despite a slow start, Finland is technologically advanced.
We could refer to advanced technology in particle research, nutrition, medicine, or steelmaking, but let us mainly consider information technology.

In the March 1999 issue of *Communications of the Association for Computing Machinery,* Kalle Lyytinen and Seymour Goodman write:

> "A nation without many natural resources, largely unsuited for advanced agriculture, [Finland] has also suffered from several wars during this century. Due to all these factors, it has historically had a relatively low economic standard of living. In 1948, Finland's GNP per capita was half of Sweden's. Traditionally, Finland's economy had wooden legs, dependent on its forests. Since World War II, Finland has developed a machine industry, which produces luxury cruisers, paper machines, and lifts. Forests and machines still account for 50% of Finland's exports, while another 25% now comes from electronics and IT. By 1997, GNP per capita equaled Sweden's."

According to the 2001 World Times Information Society Index, Finland continued in third place on the list of the world's dominant information economies. Neighbors Sweden and Norway were first and second.

A "Good Morning America" television program opened with a greeting: *"Hyvää huomenta Ameriikka!"* There were, of course, the lighter touches which showed the current competitive sports of boot-throwing and wife-carrying, but much of the program dealt with the advanced technology in Finland.

Finland has been a leader in research spending, with a goal of 2.9 percent as the share of GNP devoted to research and development. Furthermore, unlike other members of the European

Union, Finland has not cut back on research funding after joining the Union.

Surprisingly, 5.6 percent of Finland's gross national product is from computer technology. Of fifty-one nations surveyed in 1998, Finns were number one (1.5 million) in use of the Internet, twice as wired as the U.S.! Ten percent of Finns use the Internet every week to buy services or to pay bills. In 1999, it was announced that the headquarters of worldwide Internet university studies will be related to the Hämeenlinna branch of Tampere University. All residents in Finland are scheduled to have an e-mail address as well as a regular street address.

Linux, the computer operating system of Finnish origin, is gaining popularity. The system had its origin in 1991, when Linus Torvalds was a twenty-one-year-old sophomore at the University of Helsinki. He created an experimental version of the UNIX software system for students who couldn't afford Bill Gates' version. "Linus" plus "UNIX" somehow became "Linux." Free, open-source software has been developed by hundreds of volunteers linked by the Internet. With support from Netscape, that system now seems to be a rival for Windows.

Someone has remarked about the good old days back in 1850, when one could get into the bathtub and not be interrupted by a phone call for over twenty-five years, since the phone wasn't invented until 1875! Well, 3,700,000 Finns—more than 70 percent of Finland's population—have cell phones. Sophisticated cell phones with computer and fax capabilities are available. Thus, Finns can be continually interrupted by calls on the *kännykkä* wherever they are, even on the beach or in the bathroom. Finns sent over a billion cellular text messages in the year 2000, according to the Finnish Ministry of Transportation and Communications. The average cell phone subscriber sent 278 messages that year!

In Finland, cell phones are now bringing comics to users. Furthermore, Nokian Tyres include a chip that sends data on tire pressure and temperature to the driver's cell phone. In 2000, *Business Week* magazine named Finland-based Nokia as the world's top information technology company.

Finland was the first nation where income from wireless communications exceeded that from land lines. Telephone costs are among the world's lowest. Phone services are fully digitized. Ten percent of Finland's households have faxes.

Purchases by money card are common. According to the results of an international study published in 1997, Finns were the world's most active cash machine users, with the average Finn using an ATM machine forty-three times a year, compared to Swedes' thirty-three, Englishmen's twenty-five, and Germans' fifteen times per year.

Some belittlers claim that Finns are into cell phones, faxes, ATMs, and the Internet because that's easier for them than talking to real live faces, but we won't take such grumping seriously.

Communications of the ACM reported the following in its March 1999 issue: "Finland has evolved from a peripheral European country producing paper and timber into a nation with per capita IT production and use ranking among the highest in the world. In Finland, we have a rare example of a small country that is able to spawn a successful, entirely indigenous multi-billion dollar IT company." According to a 2001 survey published by the International Institute for Management Development in Lausanne, Finland was the most competitive country in the world, ahead of the United States, Canada, and Singapore. This achievement is surprising for a country that values a care-giving state. "Competitiveness" in the study is not psychological warfare but rather a measure of success in domestic economy, internationalization, government, finance, infrastructure, management, science/technology, and people.

"We salute Finland's achievements!"

THE WAIST

I am so slim,
the waist for
an hour glass.
Now through
me, past me,
the pregnant
past presses,
squeezes.
Beyond
me
history
becomes
my mystery,
futures open.
My roots are
up above me,
my branches
reach down.
I am so small.

Illustration by David Fitzsimmons